Virginia Pounds Brown

Helen Morgan Akens

ALABAMA

Mounds to Missiles

Alabama
Mounds to Missiles

By HELEN MORGAN AKENS
VIRGINIA POUNDS BROWN
Illustrated by Don Davis

THE STRODE PUBLISHERS
HUNTSVILLE, ALABAMA

Dedication

To the memory of my father, John Pounds, who with interest and enjoyment traveled throughout Alabama for over fifty years, and to my mother, Virginia Lawson Pounds.

V.P.B.

To Katherine M. Morgan and J. Martin Morgan, parents of mine and friends of Alabamians and of Alabama.

H.M.A.

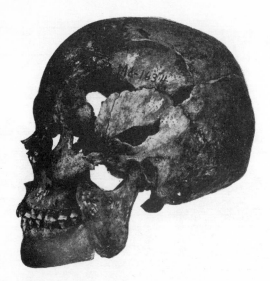

An unflattened Moundville Indian skull

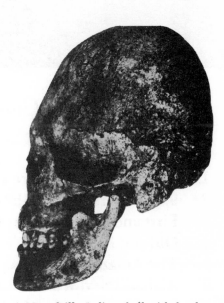

*A Moundville Indian skull with head
artificially flattened*

Mound State Monument Photo

Contents

Introduction

1. **When Flat**heads Were Famous 17
2. 9,000 Years Ago in Alabama 21
3. First and Worst Indian Battle 25
4. Old and New Mobile 30
5. The Amazing McGillivrays 36
6. Alabama Scalps and "Red Eagle" 42
7. First Students Meet in Boat Yard 55
8. Lily Flagg 58
9. Arrest of Former Vice-President 65

Introduction

CHARLES GRAYSON SUMMERSELL
HISTORY DEPARTMENT CHAIRMAN
UNIVERSITY OF ALABAMA

ALABAMA MOUNDS TO MISSILES is a fine achievement by Helen Akens and Virginia Brown. They bring into sharp focus their talents as prose writers with the production of this volume. This is notable teamwork by the two authors of Alabama history.

In some books the reader may tamely acquiesce in the authors' organization of a book beginning with page one and ending with the last page of the last signature, but it does not have to be thus in all books. Some books hang together so well that you can choose your own chapter order; and this is illustrated in ALABAMA MOUNDS TO MISSILES.

Why not read first "Lullabies and Cotton Picking" a Sumter County story? Whether or not one brings to the subject much knowledge of folk music, this short essay will surely set the right mood for best appreciation of the Akens and Brown charming volume. Or perhaps you prefer to start with the cow that became a legendary heroine. The oft-told story of Lily Flagg was never better told than here.

We should be thankful that the head flattening beauty of the Moundville Indians has not been revived except in word description. The authors of ALABAMA MOUNDS TO MISSILES give a lively description of head flattening as part of life and labor of the Indians of Moundville. Do not fail to follow Akens and Brown as they tell the story of the archeological detective work which led to the exploration of Russell Cave. Further episodes include Indian resistance to De Soto in the bloody massacre of Indians at Maubila to the massacre of whites by Indians at Fort Mims. Between the two events the spotlight centers upon Chief Tuscaloosa, the LeMoynes, the McGillivrays, Aaron Burr, Nicholas Perkins, Pushmataha, William Weatherford (the Red Eagle), and Old Hickory himself.

Yet this book has gentler tales such as the whimsical chapter on the Boat Yard School on Lake Tensas and other early schools, Colbert's Ferry and the Forks of Cypress. Here is James Jackson owner of the Forks of Cypress riding to victory on Peytona his champion horse; and there is Mrs. James Colbert dancing barefoot in a Paris hat.

One of the most fabulous careers in Alabama business was that of James R. Powell here told in striking prose. Powell worked for the pony express, riding the mails between Montgomery and Nashville. As he accumulated capital, he moved into the related business of operating stage lines and hotels. When Powell and Robert Jemison found the stagecoach business too competitive for two shrewd operators, they merged. Another among the celebrated associates of Powell was John Milner, and their joint venture was the very significant Elyton Land Company.

It was a gala day in 1880 that Birmingham people celebrated the blowing-in of the first blast furnace in Alabama. Named Alice in honor of the daughter of its owner, Henry DeBardeleben, Alabama's first blast furnace had a stack seventy-five feet high, towering over the countryside, a fitting symbol of the newly created Birmingham.

One of the most fascinating stories in this book is so much a

12

matter of atmosphere that it does not lend itself readily to summary treatment. It is enough to say here that whether or not you know the story of Rooster Bridge, do not fail to read this inviting selection.

When Frank James was tried in Huntsville, the court endeavored to sift facts from the tall tales of the notorious Frank James and his brother Jesse. Yet here, as in the other stories of Frank and Jesse, the showmen and the publicity men build a calculated smoke screen of propaganda around questions of their guilt.

When Wilbur and Orville Wright came to Montgomery in 1910 and started a flying school on land owned by Frank D. Kohn, they furnished the data for the chapter entitled "Airplanes Come to Alabama." The flying school started with only five students and ran for just a few months, but this was the start of Maxwell Air Force Base.

"The Night Von Braun Came To Dinner" ushers in the most sensational of the headline stories which these authors are so highly competent to tell. The United States could have put the world's first satellite into orbit two years before Russia instead of eighty-three days after Sputnik I. At Huntsville the modern story centers on rockets and missiles. When EXPLORER I orbited on January 31, 1958, as America's first satellite, Huntsville people danced in the streets and some celebrated all night long, for EXPLORER I was developed in Huntsville. The first sun satellite PIONEER IV (March 3, 1959) was a Huntsville product and so was the vehicle of Alan Shepard, the first astronaut (May 5, 1961).

So runs the Huntsville story furnishing this book with a title broad enough for its true scope ALABAMA MOUNDS TO MISSILES.

University, Alabama
August 1, 1962

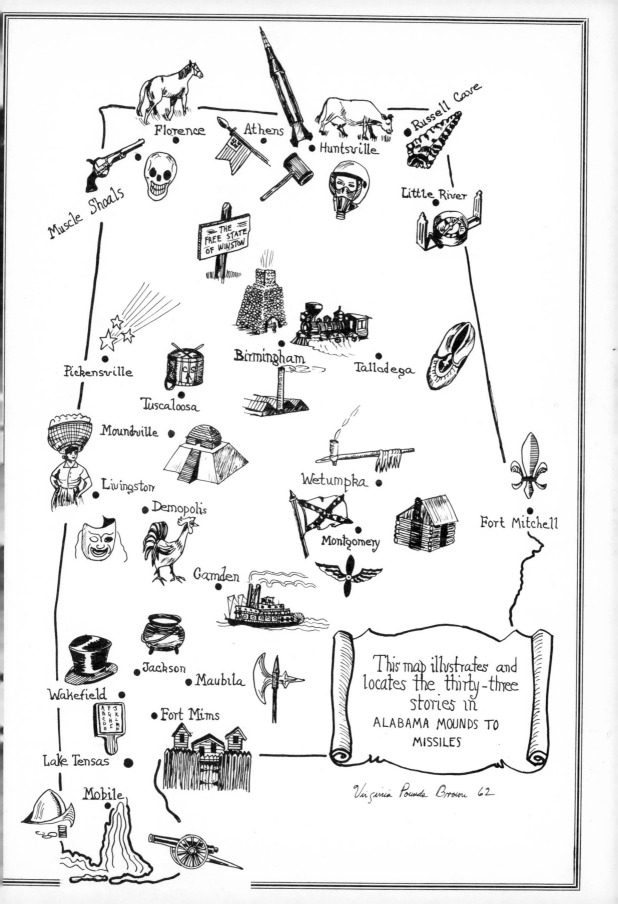

Florence
Athens
Huntsville
Russell Cave
Muscle Shoals
Little River
THE FREE STATE OF WINSTON
Pickensville
Birmingham
Talladega
Tuscaloosa
Moundville
Wetumpka
Livingston
Demopolis
Fort Mitchell
Montgomery
Camden
Jackson
Maubila
Wakefield
Fort Mims
Lake Tensas
Mobile

This map illustrates and locates the thirty-three stories in ALABAMA MOUNDS TO MISSILES

Virginia Pounds Brown 62

Diorama of Indian Village—Courtesy of Mound State Monument

Moundville was the culture center and largest city of that region

16

When Flatheads Were Famous

ONE of the strangest customs in the history of Alabama was that of head-flattening. The Indians of what is now Moundville, Alabama, went to much trouble to be sure that their children conformed to this latest fashion. They performed the art of head-flattening by strapping the infants to a wooden cradle board. The pressure of the leather thongs against the soft bones of babies' heads caused a flattening that remained through life. It was a rough way to become beautiful, but many of the Moundville Indians considered it worthwhile. A flat head seems to have been a mark of good rearing, a mark so desirable that many mothers strapped sand bags on their children's heads to cause the flattening.

Styles back then called for strange things just as they do today, but in spite of the "flathead craze" the Moundville Indians were surprisingly advanced. They appeared around the Fourteenth Century on the banks of the Black Warrior River where they constructed so many great earthen mounds they became known as the "mound builders." These mounds, built by piling one basketful of earth on top the other, are similar in many ways to the buildings of the Aztecs and Mayas.

The Moundville Indians were not warlike. They lived a pleasant and contented life, and enjoyed hunting, fishing, and farming. Their neat homes were made of logs and poles, weatherproofed with reeds and canes that were plastered with sand and clay. Swamp grass made the roof watertight, and a hole in the center served as the chimney. Moundville was the culture center and largest city of that region, making it possible for the inhabitants to live their life of relative luxury and ease. Free from the demands of making war, they developed the art of modeling and carving more than any other North American Indian.

The equipment of present-day fishermen has improved little over the Moundville Indians who used nets of vegetable fibre and barbless fishhooks of bone and copper. For hunting purposes they made artistic arrowheads for small game and ingenious traps for big game. Judging by the large and muscular physiques of the average Moundvillian, they must have eaten well.

Tobacco smoking was practiced not as a habit but as a ceremony. Pipes were carved from stone or molded from clay, and smoked through a long cane stem with a bowl resting on the ground. The dead were buried with care and respect, sometimes under the dirt floor of their own homes.

Today at Moundville, Alabama, there is a 315-acre Mound State Monument, one of the finest mound groups in the South. The tract contains forty mounds plus a restoration of several lakes probably used by the Indians for water storage and fishing supply because the lofty river bluff at Moundville's ancient river front made the Warrior River a difficult source for obtaining water. The largest mound is 58½ feet high and covers almost two acres. A modern diorama in the museum describes in picture story the surprising fact that these mounds were used primarily for the living as compared with burial mounds found at other Indian sites. Stairways on the sides of the mounds led up to temples and other important buildings on top.

Visitors to Moundville today can stand on one of these mounds and look out over the Black Warrior River a hundred feet below. On this same spot a Moundville priest may well have stood in ancient times performing a religious ceremony, the meaning of which lies buried with the "mound builders."

When he picked up a handful of arrowpoints, he wondered how they got there

9000 Years Ago In Alabama

A POWERLINE employee working near Bridgeport in Jackson County, Alabama, unearthed one of the most important archeological discoveries in North America. When he picked up a handful of arrow points, he started wondering how they got there. His curiosity led to the discovery of Russell Cave, primitive man's oldest known home in the Southeast.

It was the detective work of cave explorer Paul Brown, however, that really led to the exploration of Russell Cave. Brown, an engineer with the Tennessee Valley Authority as well as an amateur spelunker, heard about the arrow points discovered by the powerline employee. After looking at a map of the area, Brown decided that a cave on the hillside looked like a likely spot for Indians to have occupied. On weekends, Brown and a friend started digging. The two men had excavated only a few feet into the floor of the cave when they turned up pottery, shell ornaments, bone tools, and stone points. The relics were perfectly preserved and dated back to prehistoric man.

Brown reported his findings to the Tennessee Archeological Society, who explored the cave further in 1953. As the society dug deeper, they realized that Russell Cave was a major discovery and aroused the interest of the Smithsonian Institution and the National Geographic Society. In 1957 the National Geographic Society purchased the 262-acre farm on which the cave is located. They sent a professional archeologist, Carl Miller, to explore the site.

As soon as Miller arrived in Alabama and inspected the site, he drove to nearby South Pittsburg, Tennessee, and employed seven miners to dig with him. The miners, accustomed to pick and shovel, found it hard to believe that they were being paid to trowel out handfuls of dirt from carefully marked five-foot squares, six inches deep. When the miners learned, however, that each handful might contain an ancient tool or bone, they became as interested as the archaeologists themselves in seeing who could find the most. Finally, after three seasons of digging, during which three tons of dirt were sifted and removed, Russell Cave told its remarkable story of continuous use by man from prehistoric time to the Colonial Period in American history.

What was it that attracted primitive man to Russell Cave over nine thousand years ago? In the first place it was its size: a huge cave 107 feet wide and twenty-seven feet high. It was also dry. Fresh water ran at the foot of the hillside and game abounded in the forest nearby. These were all assets to primitive man, who needed easy shelter, protection from his enemies, and food to hunt. It is to the women, however, that we are indebted for the treasures of Russell Cave. These housekeepers of long ago were unbelievably messy. Instead of ridding the cave of rubbish, they simply covered it with dirt. Protected from rain, erosion, silting, and flood, the layers built up, waiting for modern man to discover this remarkable timetable of human existence in Alabama.

In 1961 the National Geographic Society presented the deed to 310 acres in Alabama to the Interior Department for the proposed establishment of a Russell Cave National Monument.

*It was unlucky for DeSoto that Tuskaloosa was not only a giant but
a shrewd giant*

First And Worst Indian Battle

THE area of Grove Hill and Thomasville and Jackson in south Alabama saw the first and bloodiest battle in North America between European white men and American Indians. In this Clarke County battle entire Indian families were burned alive in their homes. The disaster would pay bitter dividends to white families in future years.

Responsible for the Indian carnage was European adventurer, explorer, and warrior Hernandez De Soto, who marched with loud footsteps into Alabama four centuries ago and ended quietly in the waters of the Mississippi River. This army from Spain landed at Tampa Bay, and before entering Alabama went through Florida, Georgia, the Carolinas, and Tennessee. Accompanying De Soto on this exploration northward in 1540 was a strange invading force, consisting of 950 Spanish soldiers, hundreds of Indian slaves in chains, two hundred horses, and a herd of hogs that at one time numbered more than a thousand. When the army turned toward the Gulf again, it was unwelcome news to the Maubila tribe of Indians who stood between the army and its return to the Gulf's blue waters. The Maubilas were a courageous and powerful tribe, and their chief, named Tuskaloosa, was a giant of better than six and a half feet, perhaps even taller, according to De Soto's men who later told about the battle and who had reason to remember Tuskaloosa as having all the prowess claimed.

De Soto was a warrior, not a diplomat, and instead of using a peace pipe or other diplomatic gestures with Indians he met while exploring North America, he preferred to grab the Indian chief himself and make him a hostage. In doing this he hoped that the captive chief would insure safe conduct for the De Soto army, and in addition serve as guide into hidden areas where there might be gold, silver, and precious jewels. De Soto had seen such treasures in South America and was searching for similar treasures here.

It was unlucky for De Soto and his army that Chief Tuskaloosa would have preferred sitting home on his rug to accompanying De Soto from the near end of his Indian territory to the far end. It was unlucky also for De Soto that Tuskaloosa was not only a giant, but a shrewd giant, in fact so much so he remained quietly observing and making plans while De Soto's men paraded around with their heavy Spanish armor and their muskets and their lances in the Alabama autumn.

De Soto desired very much to see the famed City of Maubila, Chief Tuskaloosa's headquarters city in the interior of his Indian territory. After taking Chief Tuskaloosa captive in the northern section of his domain, De Soto requested the chief to guide his Spanish army southward to the walled city itself. To assure the chief's cooperation,

De Soto had a horse brought forward and placed Tuskaloosa on it, although he did allow the chief to ride in his own royal style on his trip south to the city. This style consisted of one of the chief's subjects holding an umbrella over his head to protect him from the Alabama sun, while other subjects walked beside him with pillows in case he desired to make himself more comfortable. But none of this today comforted the chief, for what he really desired was to be rid of his unwelcome trespassers in the land where palefaces were strangers, and as strangers were anything but welcome.

The Maubila tribe's headquarters City of Maubila lay beside a large river and must have been a beautiful place, for the area in which it stood is still scenic today. The city was really a walled fort in which the Maubila tribe could retreat for protection, and De Soto's courage or greed or both were shown by his desire to enter. The city's four walls were high and consisted of large logs, placed upright and secured by cross timbers, with interlacing foliage for additional strength. Two-story towers large enough for eight men dotted the top of the wall, and the wall itself contained only two gates, one to the east and one to the west. Crouched within this outside fortress were eighty houses, each one capable of protecting a thousand braves, women, and children, or altogether a population of eighty thousand. Lucky for De Soto the braves inside the buildings on this October morning only a few hours after sunrise were not attacking from ambush as long as their chief failed to give a signal. Lucky also for De Soto was his own decision to leave part of his army outside the fort, just in case.

This decision by De Soto proved to be one of the few really wise ones he had made since entering Tuskaloosa's domain. For inside the fort, with only part of De Soto's heavily armed warriors accompanying them, the giant chief then took himself out of the line of fire by convincing De Soto that he the chief must step into one of the buildings to pave the way for a friendly greeting from all the tribesmen. The chief's visit into the house proved to be a one way trip.

Perhaps the Indians were at first dazzled by this foreign group of armed men with strange muskets and lances, some waiting in their courtyard and others in the distance outside their fort. At any rate, time was on their side, for they were not the ones standing out in unprotected sunshine clothed in hot Spanish armor. It was De Soto and his men in this uncomfortable position. De Soto, not noted for his patience, soon grew hotter and ordered one of the chief's attendants to go in and demand the chief's return. When the Indian refused, one of the Spaniards pierced the unwilling messenger with a lance.

It was the signal for battle. Infuriated Indians began leaving the safety of the houses and descending on the De Soto army with clubs and stones. Others were armed with bows and arrows. De Soto, retreating to rally his men for a counterattack, fled toward the gate, but his heavy Spanish armor caused him to fall several times en route. He made it through and began to rally his army outside the fort, in the face of continuing Indian assault.

De Soto's armed might proved too much, and three hours

later the Indians retreated into their own trap, the stockade. De Soto forced them into their houses and then set them afire. Inside the burning houses the flames consumed women and children as well as the braves. Estimates of the Indian dead range from 2,500 to 11,000. Whatever the number lost, it was the end of the City of Maubila, and from henceforth the tribe itself was no longer a power in Alabama's Indian history. The same sunset that saw the Indians' destruction saw not more than twenty Spaniards dead, though there were "a thousand seven hundred and seventy odd treatable wounds" by actual count.

De Soto's army remained near the devastated area for three weeks, waiting for their own wounds to heal. During this inactivity, dissatisfaction grew among the men, one of De Soto's reasons for discarding his plan to reach Mobile Bay and instead "facing westward toward the unknown." This trip westward resulted in the ruin of his large army and his own burial in the Mississippi River where he, like the tribe he had massacred, faded into the shadows of history. Chief Tuskaloosa had been right in discerning early in their association that he and De Soto were not meant for each other.

Old And New Mobile

WHEN the French brothers, Iberville and Bienville LeMoyne, the founders of Mobile, sailed into beautiful Mobile Bay in 1699, they made a startling discovery. Stopping offshore at an island a few miles out in the bay from the present city of Mobile, they discovered what appeared to be a "natural mountain of bones." On closer inspection they found that it really was a huge pile of bones of Indians, both braves and squaws. It was obvious from the bones that the Indians had been beheaded—a gruesome spectacle indeed. The Frenchmen called the spot Massacre Island and later changed this name to Dauphin Island. Today Dauphin Island is a favorite resort center in the Mobile area.

The LeMoyne brothers hurriedly left the horrifying pile of bones, and continued on their way to look for a suitable location for the capital of Louisiana. Up the Mobile River, near present-day Mt. Vernon at Twenty-seven Mile Bluff, they founded Fort Louis De la Mobile. The bayou country now took on a busy atmosphere as the new capital developed. One thing, however, was lacking. Men were complaining that there were not enough women. Mobile officials wrote to their native land of France, asking for girls. In response, hurriedly departing France for the new world came the now famous "cassette girls," so called because the French government gave each girl some clothing and a small trunk called "cassette" in the French language. When the girls arrived in Mobile, they were in such great demand they had to be heavily guarded. During daylight they underwent the stares of many interested bachelors, but at night they were kept guarded by a sentry. The girls were pretty and married within a month, except for one. Some say the single reluctant bride-to-be was last to be married because she was coy. Other accounts, not quite so kind, claimed that she "looked more like a guardsman than a girl." Whatever the reason, she soon married also. In fact, with the other girls married, two men threatened to kill each other because of this reluctant girl, until the commandant of the fort made them draw straws.

The cassette girls complained about the food in the colony, especially cornbread. So loud was their complaint, it was called the "petticoat rebellion." But, all in all, the girls thrived as wives, and the first cassette child was born within a year. It became in later years very good social form to claim descent from the famous cassette girls.

In 1710, not long after the arrival of the cassette girls, the Mobile River flooded, and the fort and capital of Louisiana was moved back down the river to the present site of Mobile, although it was still called Fort Louis. Bienville had earlier settled some Choctaw Indians in this area, probably at Choctaw Point, where the Mobile River flows into Mobile Bay. With the French taking over their home sites

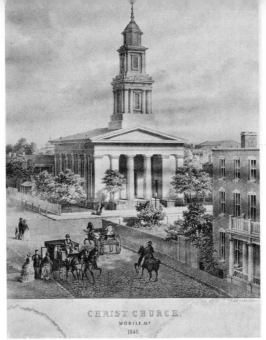

Mobile must have seemed a prize plum indeed

in present day Mobile, the Choctaws were forced to move further down the bay to Dog River.

From the beginning Mobile differed from other Alabama areas because of the French atmosphere. The streets took names that remain today as reminders of the French: Dauphin, Royal, Conti, and St. Louis. The leaders of the widespread French area centering in Mobile were of course French. The first leader had been Iberville, and then when Iberville died of yellow fever in Cuba in 1706 the mantle of leadership was taken over by his brother Bienville, who had been only eighteen years of age when he with the first Frenchmen came to the Mobile area. When Bienville succeeded his brother upon Iberville's death, he already had political experience. Bienville had founded Fort Dauphin, Fort Louis, and Mobile. It has been said that Bienville is to the Mobile area as George Washington is to the United States.

32

But Mobile had been in its present location only two years when word came from France that Bienville was to be removed as governor. Although Bienville continued to live in Mobile and later became governor again, he was succeeded by the famous Frenchman named Cadillac, for whom the Cadillac automobile is named. Even as Cadillac gave his name to the modern day automobile, Bienville's name has been associated with a modern day celebration. For it was Bienville back in 1704 who first proclaimed a Masque of St. Louis holiday for the Mobile area, the celebration which Mobilians credit as the beginning of the ever-popular Mardi Gras. The French also gave Mobile the oriental flower called the azalea, a flower for which Mobile is known as much as for its Mardi Gras.

Lucky was it that the French had made their imprint on Mobile early. For in the 1760's the French lost their claim to Mobile, the reason being a very clear-cut one. The British had taken over. Many a Mobile Frenchman must have felt a tug in his heart as the French flag dropped over Mobile and the British flag rose in its place. Some Frenchmen left town, but many stayed, and Mobile remained essentially French. The British expected much of Mobile. It was pointed out that Mobile Bay could contain "the whole British navy." Mobile must have seemed a prize plum indeed to foreign countries in the early years. The French had founded her, only to be eased out by the British in the 1760's. But then the Spanish decided that what was good enough for the French and the British was certainly good enough for them. During the American Revolution, Galvez, governor of

Spanish Louisiana, marched into Mobile. It was Britian's turn to find what it meant to lose the beautiful city on the Gulf. The Spanish stayed thirty-three years.

Mobile began to resemble a small United Nations. There were Frenchmen from the days of Iberville and Bienville. There were Mobile Britains from the momentous days of King George in the 1760's. Then there were the Spanish rulers. But of course this was not the end. During the War of 1812 some people from a place up north called the United States came in, and Mobile had found a permanent mother at last.

Mobile has continued as a small United Nations. It has a greater mixture of foreigners than anywhere else in the state. Besides being known as a cosmopolitan city, Mobile has a reputation as one of the world's biggest cotton ports of yesterday, second only to New Orleans. Long lines of wagons filled with cotton used to move through town in cotton season. Gins were busy preparing bales to line the Mobile docks. Steamboat after steamboat, flatboat after flatboat, floated down the river "gwine to ol' Mobile," as the song goes. Mobile, like New Orleans, is typical of the picturesque history of the old South. Behind the iron lace railings of its many ancient homes are shadows covering stories going back to 1540, more than four centuries ago.

*Behind the iron-lace railings of its many ancient homes are shadows
going back to 1540*

35

The Amazing McGillivrays

A STRANGER coming to Alabama might think on many occasions he was all the way across the ocean in Scotland. Few places outside Scotland have more family names of the great Highland clans than does Alabama. Especially in the southern part of the state, there is scarcely a county, or even a neighborhood, where one cannot find someone by the name of Cameron, Campbell, Ferguson, Fraser, Gordan, Graham, Morgan, McDonald, McKenzie, McIntosh, McLean, McGillivray, McLeod, McNeil, McPherson, McMillan, Stewart, or others—distinctly Highland names.

First of these Scotsmen to achieve lasting fame in the area of Alabama was Lachlan McGillivray, who came from Scotland about 1750. He started his exploration journey westward from the Atlantic seaport of Charleston, S. C. Applying his best Scottish business ability, Lachlan developed a rich trade with the Indians he met on his way. Before the Revolutionary War and the War of 1812, which broke the back of Indian resistance in the area, there were four major tribes in the area of the Mississippi Territory that would someday be Alabama. These tribes were the Creeks, Chickasaws, Choctaws, and Cherokees. Most powerful of these were the Creeks, and it was with this tribe that Lachlan did much of his trading. He soon decided that bachelorhood was not for him, and he married a French-Creek princess.

After his marriage, Lachlan left his two large plantations in Georgia for a while and settled near the Wetumpka area, in what would one day be Alabama, a few miles north of Montgomery. When the Revolutionary War started, Lachlan made the mistake of being a Tory in America; so when the British lost the war, Lachlan's immense wealth was confiscated by Americans and, in addition, they wanted his hide. Penniless and in danger of his life, Lachlan escaped to Scotland where he lived out his days, apparently quite content never to visit the New World again.

Meanwhile, at Wetumpka, Alabama, a quarter-Creek son named Alexander had been born to Lachlan and his Indian wife. Alexander became a handsome and powerful man, combining some of the best physical qualities of his Scottish father and French-Indian mother. He also received an excellent education, courtesy of his father's wealth, before his father fled to Scotland. During the Revolutionary War, Alexander had made the mistake of siding with the British, as had his father. In fact, to get Alexander's help in inciting the Indians to fight on Britain's side in the war against the Americans, the British made Alexander a colonel in the British Army and put him on their payroll. So when the British lost the war, it seemed likely that Alexander would suffer his father's fate and be chased across the ocean to Scotland.

But quarter-Creek Alexander considered himself a

Creek. He was liked by the Creeks, and because the white Americans were wary of the Creeks they did not pursue Alexander during the Revolutionary War as they had his father. As word spread that the Creeks were beginning to look upon Alexander as a "white emperor" in their midst, Americans began to consider ways to get his help in "taming" the Creeks now that the British had been defeated. In those days the Spanish also were interested in acquiring land in the area that would someday be Alabama, and they too began to try to win Alexander's favor. So Alexander started to play the Spanish against the Americans and the Americans against the Spanish, without telling his own Creek tribe what he was about, and this was how Alexander earned the reputation of being Alabama's greatest diplomat. First he had obtained money from the British, promising them the Creeks' support against the white Americans, and then after the British were defeated and his father chased to Scotland, Alexander was accepting money from both the Spanish and the Americans, promising each side the help of his Creek tribe. In June, 1784, the Spanish at Pensacola, Florida, gave Alexander a full-colonel's uniform and put him on the payroll with the title not only of colonel but also of Commissary Commissioner, the latter title intended primarily as an adornment to accompany Alexander's flashy uniform. Returning to the Wetumpka area, Alexander strutted around in his uniform of a Spanish colonel, and the Creeks considered him their "emperor" more than ever.

Then in 1787 President Washington, worried lest his infant country get into a general war with the Creeks, sent a Colonel Marinus Willett as United States emissary to the Creeks. After spending more than three months en route, the colonel finally reached Alexander McGillivray. Alexander at once sensed a new opportunity for profit when Willett told him that President Washington wanted to meet him in New York to work out a treaty with the Indians. Alexander called together various chiefs, and the strange group began accompanying Willett toward New York. First they rode horseback, but when they reached the Seneca River in South Carolina they were entertained by General Andrew Pickens who arranged for them to ride in comfortable wagons. Meanwhile, the Spanish learned of the traitorous visit to the city of New York by the Spanish colonel Alexander McGillivray, and so the Spanish sent a spy to New York with money to buy back Alexander's goodwill. The spy, perhaps asking himself what an Indian could do with all this money, may have treated himself to a New York vacation with his Spanish gold. Anyway, his Spanish gold never found Alexander, and the latter signed a treaty with General Washington on behalf of the Creek tribe. By the treaty the Creeks would not make trouble for the new government as long as Alexander received fifteen hundred dollars in gold annually and the Creek tribe itself received a few inexpensive items to keep it happy. Alexander himself would retain the rank of brigadier general in the United States government.

The United States agreed, thus giving Alexander the biggest diplomatic triumph of his amazing career. Upon returning to Wetumpka, he paraded first in his Spanish uni-

By the treaty between President Washington and Alexander Mc-
Gillivray, Alexander received fifteen hundred dollars annually

form and then in his American uniform to the delight of his Creek admirers. Yet, Alexander's happiness was short-lived. Tiring of being "played for suckers" when it became clear what Alexander was up to, both the Spanish and American governments soon disowned the Indian chief who had charged so highly for his services and done so little for them.

A few years after his return, Alexander moved to the area of Little River in the lower part of Monroe County, Alabama. There, disowned by three countries, disillusioned in the memory of his once great diplomatic career, he died, February 17, 1793. His father in Scotland had outlived his more famous son. At Alexander's death his body was taken to Pensacola for burial. The choice of burial ground was more than appropriate. For it was there, at Pensacola, that Alexander had begun his famous career of playing three world powers against each other, while he himself played at counting money from all three.

Alabama Scalps And "Red Eagle"

ONE of the most famous figures among the Indian leaders of the Alabama tribes was William "Red Eagle" Weatherford. William's tribe, the Creeks, called him Red Eagle to show their respect for his courage and fighting ability. As the name William Weatherford suggests, William was not a full-blooded Creek but was part Scottish. He too had that strain of famous Scottish blood that might have been spilled in Scotland in the mid-1700's had not its owner fled the political upheaval to come to the New World instead. Among those fleeing had been Weatherford and McGillivray, and their association continued all the way from Scotland into the area that would become Alabama. In fact, the Weatherfords and McGillivrays had married into the Creek tribe and were relatives.

By such intermarriages William Weatherford was nephew of the other most famous Scottish Alabama pioneer, Alexander McGillivray.

The relationship between William and Uncle Alexander helped them both become famous. William greatly admired his Uncle Alexander, and had done so since he was first old enough to toddle around behind him. He especially admired the way Uncle Alexander had served as leader of the Creeks and at the same time had made money from the governments of Spain, the United States, and Britain.

Before Uncle Alexander died in 1793, distrusted by Spanish and American and British governments alike for the way he had pitted them against each other, William accompanied his maneuvering uncle to Pensacola. There William watched Uncle Alexander receive weapons from the Spaniards to take home to the Creek tribe, to arm Indians to fight whites.

William, as well as Uncle Alexander, had the advantage of growing up as a rich young man in comparison with the average youth. Here in the New World the Weatherfords like the McGillivrays were able to make money by trading not only with their own tribesmen by marriage but also with Indians from other tribes, as well as with Spaniards and Americans and Britains. Alexander McGillivray's father, Lachlan, had owned two large plantations in Georgia and numerous slaves obtained by his trading acumen. William Weatherford's father, Charles Weatherford, owned a plantation and large trading store in the heart of the Creek territory, near present day Montgomery, Alabama, at the village of Coosada, just below the junction of the Coosa and Tallapoosa Rivers.

But it was not as a rich trader of mixed Indian and Scottish blood that William earned his reputation as one of the most famous among Scottish pioneers in Alabama. It was as Indian chief and warrior; it was for this that the Indians

The most famous figure among the Indian leaders of the Alabama
tribes was William "Red Eagle" Weatherford

called William Weatherford "Red Eagle." When it came to fighting, Red Eagle's heart was with the Indians' cause, not the whites', for he believed that it was wrong for the whites to come in and take the Indians' lands. Another Indian leader who felt strongly this way was Tecumseh, many years older than Red Eagle and perhaps many times more distrustful of the whites. Tecumseh came down from his Shawnee tribe in the Great Lakes area and searched out Red Eagle, urging him to delay no longer in starting a war to exterminate the whites. Partly in response to this great Shawnee chief, whose mother was from Alabama, Red Eagle in a few months gathered a thousand braves and began a "scalp hunting" journey south of Montgomery toward the Gulf.

It was not yet a full-scale war between Indians and whites, but tempers and nerves were growing taut, and little would be required to summon thousands of braves to Red Eagle's cause and thousands of settlers to the cause of the white man in settling the New World. In anticipation of full-scale war triggered by Red Eagle, the whites began building bigger and stronger forts as well as improving those already built. Such stockades were usually constructed around a group of centrally located houses overlooking the surrounding fields. A chain of these forts extended from the Tombigbee River across Clarke County and down the Alabama River to Fort Mims at Tensaw, the home of Samuel Mims, a notable old Indian trader. All this was preparation for the war that would become the famous Creek Indian War. The war itself began with the Battle of Burnt Corn near the present day boundary of Monroe and Escambia

Counties, July 27, 1813. Several hundred Indians had gone down to Pensacola for supplies and ammunition. On their way back they were attacked by territorial militiamen and volunteers under Colonel James Caller in a bend of Burnt Corn Creek. The whites routed the Indians, but in their mad rush for spoils the whites lost their advantage and were driven through the woods in confusion.

This battle infuriated the "Red Sticks," and it also gave them confidence because the whites had run. Braves, thousands of them, now took to the warpath against the whites, causing pandemonium among the settlers. In one area, the Lake Tensaw region, settlers took refuge within the unfinished walls of Fort Mims. General F. J. Claiborne, stationed at Fort Stoddert with about seven hundred men chiefly for the protection of Mobile, undertook to distribute his troops in a manner to afford the greatest protection to the people. For the defense of Fort Mims he sent 175 men under the leadership of Major Daniel Beasley, but Major Beasley weakened his small force by sending detachments to neighboring forts where citizens had congregated and were begging for help. At Fort Mims, better protected than other places, the Indians waited their chance. The people inside the fort began to think they had frightened the Indians away. The inhabitants of Fort Mims became careless. Other settlers might be getting scalped; it would not happen to them. The great gateway to the fort, which at first had been closed, now remained open not only in the day but also at night. Heavy rains had washed the sand against the gate, making it difficult to close.

*They began to think they had frightened the Indians away from
Fort Mims*

47

The fatal morning of August 30, 1813, dawned on Fort Mims, with a bright sun indicating another hot day. Male inhabitants inside the fort were lounging, some of them playing cards, others listening to a fiddler "reel off" an old tune. Women were sewing and cooking and cleaning. Some were singing. It was into a careless, carefree life such as this that the savages came shrieking on the famous summer morning of 1813. The Fort Mims massacre had begun. Before Beasley could close the gate or rally his men, the first braves were charging in past its gigantic posts. Only after a half hour of terrible fighting did Beasley manage to get the gate closed, but it was only to have Red Eagle himself now arrive at the fort with eight hundred fresh braves. Red Eagle's fresh army began throwing fire into the stockade—onto the roofs of the buildings and against the stockade logs themselves. The Indians that day took the scalps of almost 550 of the white settlers and territorial militiamen inside the fort; only a few whites managed to escape to the nearby woods. Pleading for their lives, women and children as well as men were scalped. Their dying screams finally became too much for Red Eagle. Unable to control his bloodthirsty army he withdrew from the scene of the mass murder.

The Fort Mims massacre aroused the greatest possible fear among the settlers in the Tombigbee-Alabama area, and all sought refuge in stockades. The "Red Sticks" shrieked with excitement as they pillaged the countryside, burning abandoned houses, driving off cattle, and looking for scalps.

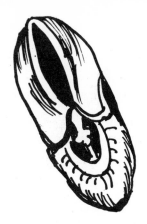

While raising troops to invade the Creek country in the Creek Indian War, Captain Sam Dale, with eighty volunteers, undertook to fight small parties of Creeks along the outskirts of the Creek domain. It was while Dale was seeking out redskins in the canebrakes that the most famous single-handed exploit of the Creek Indian War took place. On the morning of November 20, 1813, Sam Dale's scouting party saw a large canoe containing eleven Creek warriors floating down the Alabama River near Randon's Creek in Monroe County. Captain Dale and two soldiers, Jeremiah Austill and James Smith, accompanied by a free Negro named Caesar, pushed out into the Alabama River to challenge the large canoe of Indians. It was four against eleven. A few muskets were fired at close range, and Dale ordered Caesar to pull over to the Indian craft. Nobody asked for mercy, and Caesar held the two boats together while the three whites clubbed the Indians to death and threw them into the water. Because of his leadership in this fight and for other acts of courage Dale became known among the Indians as "Big Sam" Dale, and many a story round a camp-fire exploited the courage of this huge white man.

The Creek Indian War in Alabama aroused the support of the settlers in Georgia, Mississippi, and Tennessee; volunteers from all three territories joined forces with General Andrew Jackson to help the Alabama settlers. William "Red Eagle" Weatherford meanwhile had established a rendezvous for the "Red Sticks" on a bluff in the Alabama River just above Big Swamp Creek, near Powell's Ferry in Lowndes County. The place was so well fortified by nature, Indian prophets had long assured the Indians that no white man could capture it. In fact, the Indian prophets called it "Holy Ground." On December 23, 1813, the prophets were proved wrong. General F. J. Claiborne, assisted by Chief Pushmataha and other Choctaw friends, stormed the Holy Ground, killing many Indians and driving the rest into the river. Tradition has it that Red Eagle escaped by leaping his swift gray horse, Arrow, from a ten- or fifteen-foot bluff into the river, but apparently he escaped through a ravine without crossing the river. Red Eagle's disappearance in the ravine led the whites to believe that he had jumped from the bluff into the river. Claiborne could not advance further into the Creek country, for the term of his volunteers was soon to expire. He burned the town and retraced his steps by way of Fort Deposit to Fort Claiborne.

When General Claiborne returned to Fort Claiborne and General John Floyd withdrew to Fort Mitchell, the brunt of the war was left to General Andrew Jackson and the army from Tennessee. It was reported to Jackson at Fort Strother, in February 1814, that a large number of "Red Sticks" from various towns were fortified in a great bend of the Tallapoosa

*Red Eagle's disappearance led the whites to believe he had jumped
from the bluff into the river*

River—known as Horseshoe Bend—and were prepared to defend themselves at all hazards. Jackson broke camp and advanced upon them with an army of about two thousand men, many of whom were friendly Creeks, Cherokees, and other Indians. On the morning of March 27, Jackson attacked and a terrible battle surged for the remainder of the day. The Indians fought like tigers under Chief Menowa, but they were practically annihilated, while only a few white men were killed. This was the famous Battle of Horseshoe Bend that broke the power of the "Red Sticks."

Jackson, hearing that Red Eagle was rallying some of the Creeks at the Hickory Ground, marched down to the site of old Fort Toulouse, with the Indians fleeing before him. Here he established headquarters, and the fort was rechristened Fort Jackson. Delegations of Indian leaders came to the camp of "Mad Old Jackson" and surrendered. Among them was William "Red Eagle" Weatherford. While Jackson was seeking Weatherford, this fearless warrior rode into camp unattended on his old horse Arrow and surrendered. He offered himself upon the altar of revenge but begged bravely and eloquently for the Indian women and children who were starving in the woods. He even talked impudently to Jackson, but the latter was so deeply moved by Weatherford's bravery and patriotism that he forbade his men to harm him.

The story of the Indians in Alabama was concluded swiftly after the Creek Indian War that had begun in 1812. As a war indemnity the Creeks were forced to give up, by treaty of Fort Jackson, August 9, 1814, most of their domain in Alabama. William Weatherford, the former Red Eagle, and some of his followers settled in Monroe, Baldwin, and Escambia Counties, where they lived the life of pioneer farmers. They were absorbed by the whites, and their descendants today point with pride to their Indian blood, especially if they are related to William "Red Eagle" Weatherford, most famous ancestor of a number of people living near Mount Pleasant in Monroe County, Alabama.

THE SCHOOL-MASTER.

A visitor to the first school in the history of Alabama could count on quite a surprise

54

First Students Meet In Boat Yard

A VISITOR to the first school in the history of Alabama
could count on quite a surprise. Especially was this
true if his visit came during school recess. He might easily
have found himself listening to four or more languages at
once. Students in Alabama's first school included children
of English, French, Spanish, and Italian blood, and the
teacher was a Connecticut Yankee. Alabama's small pioneer
school, called the "Boat Yard School," began on Lake Tensas
about 1799. Classes were held at odd times, and on numerous occasions the students had to stay at home and work,
and so classes were not held at all. In these early years a
nine months' school term had not yet reached Alabama.

The pioneers agreed that public education was a good
thing, and one of the first important acts by the state legislature was to set aside as school property one-sixteenth of the
land in each township. This was a good start, except that
the early townships had little or no money for constructing
a school building, and even if they built one they had little
or no money for hiring a teacher. So the early settlers of
Alabama learned their three R's only by private tutors paid

for by themselves or friends. Not until 1854 were public schools in Alabama organized into a system.

Usually a church was the first building to be constructed in a new settlement; frequently this served also as a schoolhouse. The second building to be constructed was most often the log cabin school itself. Nearby was usually a blackberry patch, a shady grove for play, and an orchard from which to get switches for the cure of misbehavior. The girls swept the floor, and the boys carried water, cut wood, and made fires.

School was opened every morning with prayer and a Bible reading. The pupils recited their lessons aloud, spelling and reading in unison; they also studied aloud. Since different pupils were learning different subjects according to their ages, and since the recitations were read aloud in a single room, it is easy to understand why these early rustic one-cabin schools were called "blab" schools. The teacher of these schools was usually a young man, seldom much more learned than his oldest pupils. Nevertheless he was very strict. Nobody had any homework because the only books were owned by the teacher, who taught from Webster's spelling book, a dictionary, a geography, and McGuffey's reader.

Sometimes a large plantation owner would hire a tutor for his children, and sometimes he would even build his own school for his children. Frequently neighbor children were allowed also to attend these schools. An Englishman, Phillip Henry Gosse, who once taught in such a plantation school, wrote to his friends in London: "My schoolroom is a funny little place, built wholly of round, unhewn logs . . . there is not a window, but, as the clay has become dry, it has dropped or been punched out of many of these crevices, so that there is not want of light or air. . . . The desks are merely boards, split, not sawn, out of pine logs, unhewn and unplaned."

As communities grew and prospered, they were able to build a frame or brick school and to employ several teachers. It was a great improvement over the old-time one-room cabin. These new schools were even called academies and seminaries. The first such academy in Alabama was incorporated in 1811 by the Mississippi Territorial Legislature and was located at St. Stephens.

Of course, some people back then called the academies and seminaries a trend toward modern education, preferring instead the one-room log cabin where many voices recited aloud at the same time. But as time faded, so did these voices of regret, until today the three-R education in the cabin school can be remembered by only the older people of our generation.

Lily Flagg

WHEN John Hunt discovered in 1805 a large spring at the future site of Huntsville, Alabama, he did not know that a world championship Huntsville cow would some day rival the spring as a famous milestone in Alabama history.

As a matter of fact, Hunt and his family were much more interested in the present than in the future, especially their day-to-day encounters with huge rattlesnakes that came out in great numbers from crevices in the bluff at Big Springs. To put distance between their cabin and the snakes, the Hunt family hollowed out canes, filled them with gunpowder, and thrust them into the rocks, igniting the powder until the repeated blasts caused snakes to retreat to other crevices. Four years later, when LeRoy Pope bought much of the land surrounding the "Big Springs," suggesting that the new town be named Twickenham, he too did not know that Twickenham, Huntsville's first name, would fade into history while the name of a cow would live on as official name of an area near the springs. And a decade later, when the first governor of the state of Alabama was inaugurated in Huntsville in 1819, there was a great flow of oratory but,

*John Hunt did not know that a world championship cow would
some day rival the spring*

again, this flow of oratory could not compete in its own way
with the flow of milk that would some day descend on the city
of Huntsville in the form of a small Jersey cow.

Yes, Lily Flagg was her name, the most famous cow in
the history of Alabama, perhaps in the history of the nation.
Lily Flagg was a world champion. Like many champions,
she required several breaks before she began to make head-
lines. The pertinent facts concerning Lily Flagg's early life
are hazy, but it is known that she received her first real break
approximately in the year 1890 when she became a member
of a herd of cattle owned by General Samuel H. Moore of
Huntsville. When General Moore first bought Lily Flagg
for his dairy, she looked just like any other small Jersey cow.
But in Lily's case, the general found to his amazement that

looks were entirely deceiving. Most cows were content to give so much milk and call it a day. Not Lily Flagg. At milk time Lily was just getting started when other cows were quitting. Her milk production was tremendous. But even this was not enough. Lily was not satisfied with mere quantity. She also insisted on giving quality. In addition to producing enough milk to rival the Big Springs, week on end, Lily Flagg gave milk so rich that one could almost see the butter in it.

General Moore's amazement gave way to triumphant elation. At first almost timidly, and then more assuredly, he began to relate Lily's exploits. Soon the general's own enthusiasm was carrying him to the point where people were accusing him of exaggerating, to put it mildly. Had the sun lately been too much for the general? Was he becoming quite a bit older than he looked? It wasn't so much what the people said about him, however, that began to bother the general; it was what they said about Lily. He became infuriated. Well, the people demanded proof, so it was proof they would have. The good general would hold a contest for all the world to observe. If Lily was what he claimed, then the world had better acknowledge it.

The day of the big contest arrived, July 8, 1892. The HUNTSVILLE MERCURY, local newspaper of that day, tells this of the occasion on July 8 in Huntsville: "Wednesday afternoon, under the shade of Monte Sano, at the Monte Sano dairy, a large crowd assembled. The occasion was the finish of the greatest Jersey butter test ever known to the civilized world. . . . No pen picture can present this Jersey

60

*Lily Flagg did not even moo once although the party around her
lasted until dawn*

queen to the world . . . the most casual observer can point her out of a herd of 40 or 50 as the handsomest cow in the world." The paper goes on to state that "at 5:40 p.m. the last churning was started . . . the yield of churning was 4 pounds, 9¾ oz."

Lily's triumph appeared unquestionably to set a world's record. However, there were still some doubters, although in fairness to Huntsville it is said that few Huntsvillians if any ever doubted Lily's prowess again in General Moore's presence. As for the general himself, he of course remained proud of Lily, but he wanted yet more proof to the world outside of Huntsville.

In the fall of this same year 1892 General Moore and Lily Flagg boarded a train for Chicago, Illinois, where the general was determined to enter Lily Flagg in the Chicago World Exposition Fair. Lily walked off with every prize in her category, and at last even the Yankees publicly agreed that Lily Flagg was the greatest butter producing cow in the world.

When news of Lily's triumph in the eyes of the world reached Huntsville, there were exuberant celebrations that only people in the yesteryears knew how to enjoy, in the era before television and the automobile and good roads. But most exuberant of all of course was General Moore. This gentleman, after returning to Huntsville with champion Lily, threw a party that is still the talk of Alabama. Prominent people came from all over the country to celebrate and to honor the little Jersey who had gone to the big city and in a tremendous way had earned fame and fortune for herself and her owner. As fitting the occasion, the general had the outside of his large mansion painted a brilliant yellow. He constructed a dance platform, fifty feet square, at the rear of the house. In addition, to provide lighting, he installed the first electric lighting system in this north Alabama area.

The general was determined to repay Lily. This day

Mr. Lammel H. Moore
requests the pleasure of your company
Thursday evening, July the twenty-first
eighteen hundred and ninety two from
nine to three o'clock
   Huntsville, Alabama
    Complimentary
     to
Signals Lily Flagg the Jersey Cow of the World
  One year's record
 Butter 1,047 pounds, ¾ ounces.
  Milk 11,339 pounds
Winner of the Derby of the Jerseys against
 the great Bissons' Bells
   Record
 Butter 1028 pounds 15 ⅜ ounces
  Milk 8412 pounds 7 ounces
R.S.V.P.

Prominent people all over the country accepted their engraved invitations to celebrate and honor the little Jersey

was for her.   No longer were people accusing him of having stayed out in the sun too long.   Lily had proved that the general's word was still the word of an officer and a gentleman.   For this occasion too he had thousands of flowers beautifying his mansion and grounds.   And on the front lawn, waiting to welcome her guests, was who else but champion Lily Flagg herself, standing relaxed in her stall, a stall completely covered with roses.   The Italian orchestra began sending soft music through the night air.   The party grew loud with laughter and gaiety. On this night General Moore, who was a bachelor, was said to have imbibed quite a bit, and promenaded more than one Southern belle across the dance floor.   Everyone was hilarious except for the champion herself. After the party really got under way, Lily stood silent and alone out on the front lawn, munching hay in her stall.

She did not even moo once, although the party around her lasted until dawn, and by that time of course Lily had a right to sound off, if did anyone.

Today a store and gin and various residences comprise the community of Lily Flagg in south Huntsville. Some of the old-timers still gather regularly for checkers in the gin office, and between moves they sometimes talk about the cow for which the community is named. Across town is the plantation-type home, occupied by the Milton K. Cummings family, where the party for Lily occurred. It is between the Cummings' home and the checker game that occurred those momentous occasions when Lily Flagg proudly strolled along Huntsville paths, her head high, her eyes alert, her place in history assured.

Arrest Of Former Vice-President

A N EVENT of national concern occurred in Alabama in 1807 when Aaron Burr, former United States Vice-President, was arrested for treason near Wakefield in present-day Alabama, Washington County. Burr, heavily disguised, had escaped federal authorities in Natchez, Mississippi, where he was being held for trial after his unsuccessful attempt to lead a rebellion against the United States. As he fled from Natchez, this troubled man, who first became unpopular for killing Alexander Hamilton in a duel, wondered frantically where he might hide. He decided to try to reach the home of Colonel John Hinson on the Tombigbee River near Wakefield. Perhaps Hinson would hide him. Burr had met Hinson several months before in Natchez, and Hinson had seemed so captivated by Burr's magnetic personality he had offered the hospitality of his home should Burr ever be in Washington County, then part of the Mississippi Territory.

Late in the evening of February 18, 1807, Burr made the costly mistake of stopping at a cabin near Wakefield to ask directions to Colonel Hinson's place. Two men, play-

Late in the evening Aaron Burr made the mistake of asking directions

ing backgammon there, gave directions in reply to Burr's inquiry. No sooner were the travelers out of sight than one of the men, Nicholas Perkins, a lawyer, turned to his companion and said, "That man is Aaron Burr wanted for treason by the United States government. I have read a description of him, and it fits perfectly. We must find the sheriff and have Burr arrested."

The sheriff, however, could not bring himself to arrest a former Vice-President of the United States, but persistent Perkins summoned Captain Edward P. Gaines from nearby Fort Stoddard. Gaines with a file of mounted soldiers caught up with Burr and his companion the next morning soon after they left Colonel Hinson's house. He arrested him in the name of the United States government and took him as a prisoner to Fort Stoddard.

The arrest of Aaron Burr was easy compared to the task of returning him to Federal authorities in Washington. A thousand miles had to be crossed, and many sympathizers of Burr stood ready along the way to free him if given the chance. Captain Gaines put Nicholas Perkins in command of the eight men carefully picked for the difficult journey. In early March, 1807, the heavily armed little band set out, traveling sometimes by water, sometimes by horseback. One month later the group arrived in Richmond, where Burr was turned over to the proper authorities.

Only once did Burr try to escape, and that was while passing through Chester District, South Carolina, where his son-in-law lived. Burr spotted a group of men and suddenly threw himself from his horse shouting, "I am Aaron Burr under military arrest and claim the protection of the civil authorities.'' Perkins with a pistol in each hand demanded that Burr remount. When he refused, Perkins dropped his pistols, seized Burr around the waist, and threw him back into the saddle. The party was out of sight before the group of South Carolinians knew what had happened.

The Federal government was indeed grateful to Nicholas Perkins of Washington County for the important part he played not only in the capture of Aaron Burr but also in the difficult task of taking him as a prisoner from Alabama to Virginia.

Diving For Treasures

GAIETY and music plied the waters of the Tombigbee and Alabama Rivers a hundred years ago. Carefree crowds danced and sang in boats on the rivers except on those memorable occasions when overheated boilers exploded, causing men, women, and children to drown in each other's arms as fires burned around them on open water.

From the time Alabama became a territory in 1812 until the railroad era began after the Civil War, about five hundred side-wheelers plied the state's waters. Alabama soon had its own boat-building industry, with a large boat appropriately named the ALABAMA as the first one constructed inside the territory, in 1818 near old St. Stephens. The banks of the Tombigbee and Alabama Rivers were dotted with more than 450 boat landings along their winding lengths during this first half of the Nineteenth Century. These landings contained passengers and freight or sometimes merely stacks of wood, where steamers would heave to and feed their hungry, temperamental, and often murderous boilers. Life on Alabama rivers, with calliopes playing and passengers dancing and singing, often ended in catastrophe as entire ships exploded and sank, sometimes

One of numerous tragic boat accidents during the era was that of the good ship ORLINE ST. JOHN

in sight of boat landings crowded with waiting friends and relatives.

One of numerous tragic boat accidents during this era was that of the good ship ORLINE ST. JOHN. Today, a century after the accident, a storekeeper at Possum Bend near Camden, Alabama, is filling one of his cabinets with treasure from the sunken ship. The storekeeper, Mr. William Harris, is a former mariner long familiar with river and ocean currents, and he and some helpers dive into the Alabama currents at low ebb in late summer to bring up coins and other valuables from the ORLINE ST. JOHN not far under water. In low water the hull of the ship is visible from the surface of the river. There have been estimates that as much as a quarter of a million dollars went down with the ORLINE ST. JOHN on that memorable day, March 6, 1850. It was a bizarre tragedy, similar to many steamboat accidents in those days, with bodies finding watery graves at no great distance from the shore. In those days not so many people could swim, apparently, and there was in addition much fear that a burning steamboat would soon explode, a fear causing some of the people to stampede.

After the first frantic yell of "fire in the wood room," a wild evacuation began. A carpenter and some other men grabbed the ship's only lifeboat and started toward shore, leaving the rest of the passengers to swim or drown. So great was the hysteria on the ORLINE ST. JOHN, some men jumped from the boat's low deck into the whirling boat's path, to be swept under and drowned as the boat's captain sought to guide it to shore. A terrified woman leaped with such haste her dress was caught, and she was held suspended

71

for a while before dropping to her death in the water. A few people remained calm enough to try to save some of their possessions as well as themselves. On the ORLINE ST. JOHN there was gold in large quantity. In those days, without ready access to checking accounts or even paper currency, people often transported large sums of money in gold. This was true on the ORLINE ST. JOHN. Amid the hysteria around him a Navy purser from California lost track of a trunk of gold he was transporting, and a friend attempted to save it, either for the purser or himself. He got as far as the ladies' cabin, where the flames forced him to abandon his plan and swim for shore.

Storekeeper Harris's attempts to find gold in the river bed are based on newspaper accounts of the ship's destruction. The MOBILE DAILY ADVERTISER estimated the loss at fifteen thousand dollars in gold, but a passenger's letter in the GREENSBORO BEACON days after the disaster stated that two California merchants were carrying $500,000 in gold. Other sources estimated an additional sixteen thousand dollars in gold dust in the vessel's safe. But one newspaper account in particular inspires merchant Harris to continue searching for gold at the scene of the tragedy 2½ miles above Bridgeport in Wilcox County. This was a notice in the MOBILE DAILY ADVERTISER two days after the ship went down, March 8, stating that "any person who may be so fortunate as to secure any of this valuable property is entitled to salvage."

Harris has not yet found any real treasure, but he has brought up items ranging from stray gold pieces to knives and scissors and other merchandise that have been buried in

*Overheated boilers exploded, causing men, women, and children
to drown in each other's arms*

73

water for 112 years. Meanwhile, at the end of each summer, when the river is low, Harris and his helpers dive down and look around.

Because of the many steamboat accidents in Alabama before the time of the railroad, there must be many historic items resting on the bottom of Alabama rivers. A story in an Alabama newspaper in 1826 announced "with extreme regret . . . the loss of another steamboat . . . the ALA-BAMA." A third example of the numerous steamboat losses was ELIZA BATTLE. The account of that tragedy, in the CLARKE COUNTY DEMOCRAT of March 11, 1858, is interesting not only for its history but for its example of newspaper writing in the Nineteenth Century.

BURNING OF ELIZA BATTLE

The news was brought this morning, (says the Mobile *Tribune* of the 4th inst.) of a terrible steamboat disaster, on the Bigbee River, last Monday morning. Some 30 or 40 lives were lost, and over 1200 bales of cotton destroyed. Nothing except the hull of the boat was unconsumed.

The following particulars we have gathered from various sources, and we publish them in extra form, for the purpose of relieving the intense excitement which is universally felt on the subject.

The deaths resulted principally from the cold. Many of the terrified passengers escaped on cotton bales—some of them were drowned—others swam to the trees, and were found there clinging to the branches, some at the point of death, and some were actually frozen stiff. It is a shocking calamity.

About 2 o'clock on the morning of the 1st inst., the steamer *Eliza Battle*, Captain S. G. Stone, was observed to be on fire in the after part of the boat. The tiller rope was immediately burnt, with the flames running with fearful rapidity at once communicated with the ladies cabin, thus cutting off all connections with the life boat and yawl. . . .

One child of Mr. Cromwell was saved by Mr. Frank Stone, 2d clerk of the boat, who swam ashore with it. He then placed Miss Turner on a cotton bale and safely landed her on shore. She said to him, "You have saved my life; do save my mother and my sister." He then swam off and rescued her sister who froze to death in his arms. Her mother froze to death on a tree, which was the fate of almost all who perished. . . .

74

Partly because of the steamboat accidents and in part because of cheaper rates, some people still preferred to travel the river on rafts or flatboats. This means of travel, when not floating downstream, required pushing with poles or pulling with ropes thrown around trees, but at least there were no engines to cause fires and explosions, and certainly it was the economical way to travel. Usually these rafts or flatboats floated on two large slabs of well-seasoned timber held together by a floor of roughhewn slabs. This entire floating structure was built so that it could resist all shocks of driftwood or projecting rocks. The floor was caulked with tar to make it waterproof from below, and a roof was overhead to protect from rain as well as from the hot Alabama sun. In many ways these flatboats were the most pleasant way to travel in the early half of the Nineteenth Century. True, if one travelled upstream, the poling and pulling by ropes was difficult and time consuming, requiring as long as three months to go from Mobile up to Montgomery. But it was leisurely living, either upstream or down. Even the songs of the travellers suggested happiness: "Gwine down to big Mobile, so row, boatman, row."

The ORLINE ST. JOHN, the ALABAMA, and the ELIZA BATTLE could sink and leave all the treasures they desired on the bottom of Alabama rivers. The flatboats would float gently along amid the best of the good life, leaving their treasures primarily in the form of nostalgic memories of floating leaves and gentle winds along the hundreds of miles of Alabama waterways.

The Land Boom That Backfired

THE great Alabama migration of 1817-1818 brought not only homesteaders but also speculators to claim the public land formerly owned by the Indians. As soon as the land was surveyed, the government announced it for sale at public auction. It was necessary to pay only a small down payment on the purchase price of land, and this could be paid in bank notes that were frequently worth less than the paper they were printed on. The speculators formed land companies that bought up large tracts of land that they had never seen. At the land sales at Huntsville in 1818, prices soared to fantastic heights as the companies bid against each other.

Many a homesteader found that the land he had cleared and now claimed by squatters' rights had been bought from under him by one of these companies. Even if he made the trip to Montgomery or Huntsville to bid at the auction, he could not compete with the bids of the land speculators. In many cases, he found it cheaper to pay the speculator hush money so that he would not bid against him.

By 1820 the State Legislature abolished the "buy now, pay later" system but not before Alabamians had gone into

—From Collection of Alabama Pioneer Pictures in The Huntsville Times

*He found it cheaper to pay the speculator hush money so he would
not bid against him*

debt for eleven million dollars' worth of land, according to
price. Although the 1820 legislative act in Alabama ended
the famous land boom, memories of bitterness against Alabama's land speculators continued for many years, and in
some cases the ill will created then is felt today between
classes of people.

*James Jackson's horse Peytona won the right to represent the South
and the Forks of Cypress*

Forks Of Cypress

THE Forks of Cypress, a plantation that stands today a few miles out of Florence, Alabama, was a hundred years ago the center of famous racing horses in the bluegrass region of the Tennessee Valley. Traces of the once famous track which circled the meadow in front of the house are still evident. It was here that the owner and builder of the Forks, James Jackson, realized his dream of owning a string of thoroughbreds that were as good as any in the world of his day.

An Irishman by birth, Jackson came as a young man to Nashville, Tennessee, seeking his fortune. His inborn love of horses attracted him to Andrew Jackson, whose pastime was horse racing, a favorite sport of many planters and their wives in the old South. James Jackson spent many hours at the track at the Hermitage, Andrew Jackson's plantation in Nashville, Tennessee. With the help of Andrew Jackson, who was mainly responsible for opening up Indian lands in Alabama for settlement, James Jackson formed the Cypress Land Company and made a fortune in the land boom of 1818 and 1819. It was James Jackson's company which laid out the city of Florence, Alabama.

In 1820 James Jackson selected a site of three thousand acres six miles from Florence to build his own home and to start his stock farm. He built one of the most beautiful mansions in Alabama, a house noted for its colonnaded veranda extending around all four sides. Soon a regulation race track appeared in the flat meadow below the hill on which the house still stands. The Forks resounded with gaiety as famous visitors came from all over the country to race their thoroughbreds with Jackson and to enjoy the hospitality of his family.

In 1835 Jackson sent his buyer to England with instructions to buy the best horse on the market regardless of price. That horse was Glencoe, once owned by King George IV. It took fifty-two days of careful traveling to bring Glencoe to the United States. He was rested for several days in Virginia before making the final trip over the mountains into Alabama.

The most famous race of ante-bellum days, comparable to the present-day Kentucky Derby, was held at the Union Track, Long Island, New York. There the champion of the South met the champion of the East in yearly competition. In 1845 Jackson's horse, Peytona, direct descendant of Glencoe, won the right to represent the South against the East at Long Island. In May of that year a record Long Island crowd of over 120,000 people watched the South's representative, Peytona, nose-out the Eastern champion, Fashion.

Coming forward to receive the winner's trophy on that proud day for Southern planters was James Jackson of the Forks of Cypress, Florence, **Alabama.**

Colbert's Ferry On The Natchez Trace

TRAVEL on the Natchez Trace was risky business in pioneer days. Formerly an Indian trail no wider than two horses, the Trace stretched 550 miles through unprotected wilderness between Nashville and Natchez. Two days out of Nashville the Trace crossed the Tennessee River where Muscle Shoals, Alabama, is today. There a Chickasaw Chieftain, James Colbert, operated a ferry. He was assisted by innumerable members of his tribe, who received their pay in whiskey. After ferrying the weary passengers across the river, Chieftain Colbert with an eye to further business provided shelter and food at a crude inn. The bed was likely to be in a cabin with fifty or more Indians but the food of venison, potatoes, and coffee was ample. Mrs. Colbert, wife of the chieftain, sometimes entertained her husband's customers by dancing barefoot, wearing a Paris hat.

Many travelers on the Trace were traders from Kentucky and Tennessee coming up from Natchez and New Orleans on the return trip home. They were taking the easier overland road rather than fighting the upstream river currents.

These traders were ripe subjects for robbery and murder

These traders, their saddlebags bulging with money from their sales, were ripe subjects for robbery and murder. Outlaws like John Murrell, noted for his genteel manners and fast pistol, would slit a traveler's throat for a fine horse or a hundred dollars. Woe to the traveler who thought to hide his earnings in the woods before camping for the night. He frequently was killed for his trouble.

In spite of having to sleep with fifty Indians or having to sit around and observe Mrs. Colbert dance barefoot in a Paris hat, the average traveler counted it lucky indeed to spend a night's lodging on the Natchez Trace at James Colbert's ferry, two days out of Nashville.

Alabama's First World-Famous Visitor

ALABAMA cannot claim that George Washington slept here, but it can claim that another world-renowned figure did so, and this person in his day was even more famous than Washington himself. He was General Marquis de Lafayette, the famous Frenchman who helped George Washington and his young United States win the Revolutionary War, freeing this country from British rule. On his triumphal tour of the United States in 1824-25 Lafayette listened to the persuasive tongue of Governor Israel Pickens of Alabama, who wanted the general to take the overland route to New Orleans. This would bring him across Alabama, thus honoring the six-year-old state with an official visit. Early in April of 1825 Lafayette, accompanied by his son and a secretary, made a week of one-night stands through Alabama, and did so amid such official ceremony that it has not been forgotten since.

His first landing in present-day Alabama, then part of the Creek Nation, must have been a surprise to the sixty-eight-year-old nobleman. As the barge on which he ferried across the Chattahoochee to Alabama touched the banks at Fort Mitchell, the general, sitting sedately in his large car-

Special beds and chairs were imported for General LaFayette's comfort

riage, found himself surrounded by fifty shouting Creek Indians. These had been gathered there by the whites to welcome "the great white father" to their Indian land that would someday be added to Alabama. The savages grabbed the drag ropes of the carriage and pulled it and the general "in a most abrupt manner" up the bank from the ferryboat. It must have been a thoroughly surprised general who met the august Alabama delegation waiting on the bank with instructions from Governor Pickens to escort Lafayette through Indian territory to the new state of Alabama, still an infant in size and age.

After a colorful game of ball staged by the Indians on the banks of the river, the two-day trek through the Creek Nation on the old Federal Road got underway. Lafayette, now riding in a state-furnished carriage drawn by four white horses, was accompanied by two troops of state militia and at least one hundred Indians who followed with bows, arrows, and tomahawks. The Federal Road hadn't seen such activity since the Indian Wars, and wasn't prepared for it. At a point where a bridge was awash from heavy spring rains the Indians stood waist deep in the water with arms locked to make the way for the procession. At designated resting places, food had been sent ahead and awaited the party. Even special beds and chairs were imported for the general's comfort. At Line Creek, the boundary of the Creek Nation, the Indians reluctantly turned back, leaving the whites to carry the general into the area that was then Alabama.

Like the state of Alabama, the city of Montgomery at

that time was only six years old. Andrew Dexter and John Scott, who had founded separate adjoining towns called "East Alabama" and "New Philadelphia," had formed these as one town in 1819 and called it Montgomery. When Lafayette rode into Montgomery on April 3, 1825, every citizen of the town and many from the surrounding area gathered to greet this national hero, especially famous now as the only surviving general of the Revolutionary War. Congressman Bolling Hall led the procession up Goat Hill, where the capitol stands today, as the band played "Hail to the Chief." He presented Lafayette to Governor Israel Pickens, who had come from Cahaba, then the state capital, to give official greetings to Lafayette. When the time came for Governor Pickens to speak, he was so overcome with emotion he could not say a word.

The people of Alabama could not find enough ways to express their genuine affection for this Frenchman who had contributed so much to the United States' cause in the Revolutionary War. They came hundreds of miles—on foot, in ox carts, on horseback—to catch a glimpse of Lafayette and to hold up their children for him to bless. Everyone felt that the seventeen thousand dollars appropriated by the Alabama Legislature for his whirlwind tour of the state was well spent.

*Behind them lay the "Trail of Tears" marked with the many graves
of the old and sick*

Trail Of Tears

HISTORY is filled with famous death marches, but few equal in sadness the exodus of the Alabama Indians from their ancestral land to their new home in the Territory of Oklahoma. Between 1830-1840 there was a final glimpse of the Indians of Alabama. "Like the leaves of the sycamore when the wind of winter is blowing," mourned a Choctaw orator, "the Indians are passing away, and the white people will soon know no more of them than they do of those deep caves out of which they had their origin!"

In 1832 the Creek and Chickasaw Indians ceded to the United States all right to their territory east of the Mississippi River. In 1835 the Cherokees gave up most of their land when they signed the Echota Treaty, and in 1838 by the Dancing Rabbit Treaty the Choctaws relinquished all of their holdings in Alabama and Mississippi. Some of the wealthier Indians were allowed to remain, but most of them were sent west at different times and by different routes. There are many accounts of pioneer Alabamians who remember seeing the Indians sorrowfully pass their homes on their long walk.

89

One of the great moments in Alabama oratory occurred when Chief Eufaula made a farewell address to the State Legislature as he passed through Tuscaloosa on his way west. Rising with a profound dignity, he stood upon the rostrum and with no malice toward the white man spoke these words: "I come, Brothers, to see the great house of Alabama and the men that make the laws, and to say farewell in brotherly kindness before I go to the far West where my people are now going. . . . We leave behind our good will to the people of Alabama. . . . I come to say farewell to the wise men who make the laws, and to wish them peace and happiness in the country which my forefathers owned, and which I now leave to go to other homes in the West. I leave the graves of my fathers . . . but the Indian fires are going out . . . and new fires are lighting there for us."

One of the best documented marches along the "Trail of Tears" was that of one group of Creeks which began on a hot day in August, 1836, near Talladega, Alabama. About 1,170 Creeks had been assembled in a field with three hundred guards assigned to keep them quiet. There were women, children, and old people as well as the warriors of the tribe. They had brought all of their worldly possessions with them to carry to their new home. This group was marched to Gunter's Landing on the Tennessee River, where they waited while most of their guards returned to herd another 2,320 Indians to join the original party. After ninety-three days the refugees arrived in Indian Territory, greatly decreased in number.

The Alabama Emigration Company was responsible for

providing food and water for the long march, but frequently both were scarce as the company did not carry supplies with it but depended upon the countryside to provide. In the cold November weather, the Indians were hard put to make the clothing which had served them in Alabama's warm August do against the bitter winter winds of the West. As most of the thousands were on foot, carrying or dragging behind them their possessions, their moccasins quickly wore out and there were no replacements. However, they averaged twelve miles a day, prodded along by the many guards.

When they arrived in the Territory of Oklahoma, most of them were barefooted—that is, those who had survived the long march. Behind them lay the "Trail of Tears" marked with the many graves of the old and sick who could not make it to the new land.

In their new land, however, a number of these Indians received oil for their wounds—literally. Gushers of oil from the bowels of earth flowed into pipelines, turning eventually into money. This money then came to bless the destitute pockets of many a former Alabama Indian on an Oklahoma reservation.

It was a sleepless night for many an Alabamian who spent the hours gazing at the sky in terror

The Night The Stars Fell On Alabama

ASTRONOMY books and newspapers leave no doubt that stars literally "showered" the state of Alabama on November 13, 1833, with the most brilliant display of meteors in the history of the world. It was a sleepless night for many an Alabamian who spent the hours from midnight to dawn gazing at the sky in terror. Some terrified observers spent considerable time making amends with their conscience. One such group consisted of a party of young men playing cards in the Fayette County Courthouse when the stars began to fall. Their interest in their game is said to have waned considerably as star after star began falling their way. Could this be the hand of God, chastising them for their sins? Their answer to the question is not certain, but it is certain that they began to run. And when their feet would not move them fast enough, they left on their horses, and when their horses were too slow for their liking, it is said they did everything but leap off and push, to make them move faster. And since there was no escaping the brilliant, falling objects, the young men decided they should indeed repent of their sins. A Methodist minister lived a quarter of a mile from Fayette, and thenceward on their horses they sped. They arrived at the minister's home at last, and a scene of great repentance occurred. The youths promised the minister they would forever forsake card games if his prayers would but save them from destruction on this horrifying night. So the minister prayed, and all lived to see a new day.

However, despite their promises to the contrary, the young men were evidently compulsive gamblers. By Saturday night a card game was once more in progress in the Fayette County Courthouse, but, according to newspaper accounts, between shuffles of the cards more than one eye glanced heavenward, and the owners of the glances were not necessarily praying.

A similar time of repentance occurred among a group near Huntsville. The frightened group in this case consisted not of youth but of Tennessee Valley gentlemen who were gathered at the Pulaski Pike Race Track for their annual week's holiday of horse racing, cock fighting, and card playing. On the night of November 13th a card game was in full swing about midnight when one of the servants came rushing into the house, shouting that judgement day had come. One look at the sky convinced the men that it was indeed the end of the world. The poker game broke up in wild confusion as the planters crawled under tables, chairs, and beds. Those who couldn't find anything to crawl under covered their heads with their coats and squatted in the corner.

Of course, fear that night was not limited to those with guilty consciences.

John Anthony Winston, destined to be the first native-born governor of Alabama, and his cousin, William Winston, decided to pitch camp near Pickensville on that memorable night. They had left Mississippi before dawn hoping to reach their homes in Sumter County by night, but the weather was unseasonably warm and the horses had not made good time. These two pioneer settlers of the Choctaw country knew the land well, and they made camp in a familiar clearing by Fire Creek. John Winston had things on his mind, and at midnight he was still tossing in his blanket, wide-eyed and sleepless. As he lay gazing up into the sky, he was suddenly aware that streams of light were beginning to appear and disappear in every corner of the sky. He did not immediately arouse his cousin, thinking that it was just a few shooting stars that would soon disappear. But each minute the heavens became more brilliant. Winston leapt to his feet, calling to William that "the heavens are on fire."

This shower of the Leonids was seen all over North America, but it was particularly brilliant in the southeastern states. Edmund Ruffin of Richmond, awakened by a terrified servant just before daybreak, testified that streams of light, shooting like rockets, covered the sky. An observer in Augusta, Georgia, said the stars descended to the earth like a snow storm.

The science of meteoric astronomy dates from this unique display of 1833. One astronomer estimated that ten thousand meteors fell in one hour. A Yale professor said one meteor that he observed was as large as the moon and that the flashes of light were so bright as to awaken people in their beds. The shower started about midnight and lasted until the light of the sun brightened the sky. In Alabama the maximum shower was between 2:30 a.m. and 4:00 a.m.

Although it is easy to laugh about it more than a hundred years later, if modern day Alabamians should awaken some night to a sky filled with falling stars, there undoubtedly would be much activity resembling a night in 1833.

Tippecanoe And Montgomery Too

WILLIAM HENRY HARRISON, destined to serve as President of the United States for only one month, once brought a log cabin to Montgomery, Alabama, and gave it as a gift to one of his admirers. This was during Harrison's 1840 campaign for the presidency, when he traveled around the nation in a log cabin mounted on a wagon pulled by oxen. Campaigning with the slogan "Tippecanoe and Tyler too," General Harrison represented himself as a sturdy son of the frontier and a simple man of the people. By the time he reached Montgomery, however, this rough means of travel had become too much for the sixty-eight-year-old Harrison. Realizing that he needed medical attention, he called Dr. Thomas Brown, who lived on a plantation a few miles east of Montgomery.

Dr. Brown took one look at Harrison and said, "I am taking you to my plantation for a complete rest—log cabin, oxen, and all."

Harrison regained enough strength to be driven into Montgomery in Dr. Brown's carriage to make a few public appearances, but he knew he must abandon any further idea of campaigning in his log cabin. One day as he and Dr.

Yet none of them can claim the distinction of having arrived in the state behind a pair of oxen

Brown drove into the plantation, Dr. Brown's daughter came running to greet them. Harrison smiled down at her and said, "Mary Eliza, how would you like my cabin for your playhouse? I'll fit it out for you with just the right size furniture."

Harrison was true to his promise, and Mary Eliza Brown enjoyed for many years this reminder of "Tippecanoe and Tyler too."

Harrison's visit to Montgomery occurred at a time when Alabama's center of population was shifting heavily toward this central Alabama city, a fact interesting of course to political candidates seeking votes. When the capital was moved to Montgomery in 1847 from Tuscaloosa, a prophecy was fulfilled. An early Montgomerian named Andrew Dexter had set aside Goat Hill with the prophecy that one day the capitol of the state would be built on this spot. Dexter in his optimism had not foreseen that Montgomery in 1847 would be selected as the capital of Alabama. So close was the selection between Montgomery and Wetumpka, the state legislature took sixteen ballots to decide, and Montgomery won by only three votes. It was claimed by some that Montgomerians swayed the voting by distributing among the legislators a menu of the good food available at the Exchange Hotel in Montgomery.

In the years after the capitol came to Goat Hill, Montgomery received other Presidents or future Presidents as guests in addition to William Henry Harrison. These included Martin Van Buren, Millard Fillmore, James K. Polk, Grover Cleveland, Theodore Roosevelt, and Franklin D. Roosevelt.

Today the capitol building in Montgomery, patterned after the national Capitol, is an imposing example of the Greek Revival architecture so popular in the pre-Civil War South. Its ninety-seven-foot dome can be seen for many blocks down Dexter Avenue as well as in other areas of the city. Surrounding the building are impressive lawns with many azaleas, camellias, and dogwood trees. A garden on the south lawn has such a variety of roses that some are in bloom every month of the year. Visitors can stand on the brass star on the front portico of the capitol, a star that marks the spot where Jefferson Davis was inaugurated as President of the Confederacy. Across the street is the Little White House where Davis lived during his brief stay in Montgomery.

Also on Capitol Hill is the Department of Archives and History established through the efforts of Thomas McAdory Owen, who served as first Director of the Department and who was succeeded by his widow, Marie Bankhead Owen. Here the visitor may see relics that go back many years, from the time of the Indians who built burial mounds in Alabama to the time today when space activities abound in the state. A particular treasure of the department is a piece of wallpaper secured from France which shows the Vine and Olive Colony refugees busy at work building their cabins at Demopolis.

Yet, as historic as these Demopolis cabins are, none of them can claim the distinction of having arrived in the state behind a pair of oxen, to be presented to an admirer of a future President of our nation.

Masks And Lighted Torches

IN Alabama today few old-world celebrations are remembered, but in Livingston, Alabama, there is one celebration as much alive as it was a hundred years ago. Its purpose is to mark the end of the old year and the beginning of the new by a masquerade procession of men and boys, which moves by torch-light through Livingston on New Year's Eve. Any man or boy resident of Livingston or anyone visiting there on New Year's Eve is eligible to participate.

It is generally believed that the celebration goes back to the Middle Ages when in northern England and Scotland it was the custom to celebrate the Feast of Fools by masquerade processions. By means of these masquerades the people could express their opinion of their lords and were allowed certain liberties not permitted at other times. Settlers from Scotland brought this custom to North Carolina, and their descendants who settled in Livingston carried on the tradition. Colonel Thomas Wetmore is the gentleman generally credited with starting this celebration in Livingston in the 1840's.

At first the organization was known as "The Indom-

Many generations of natives and visitors to Livingston will never forget the sight of masked figures

itables." Somehow this name became corrupted to D.U.D.'s, the name by which it goes today. Though the D.U.D.'s operate without a formal organization of officers and regulations, they usually have a leader who is recognized by common consent. One of the most picturesque leaders was W. S. Nichols. He performed his traditional duties without any formal instructions and entirely voluntarily, placing signs about town announcing the hour of march and the place. He would see that the torches, at first blazing pine knots and later kerosene oil torches, were prepared and taken to the meeting place. He would also determine the line of march and assume responsibility for keeping order. He was the final authority on the route of the procession and usually led it, either followed or preceded by two drummers.

Amid the beat-beat of the D.U.D. drums, the crowd gathers at the famous Bored Well in the Courthouse Square. There they see in review those taking part in the parade. The judges make their decisions and prizes are awarded for the costumes. Masks are removed and the identity of each parader is made known to the public.

This traditional way of marking the end of the old year and the beginning of the new is looked forward to by many visitors as well as citizens of Livingston, both young and old. The children delight in it and are encouraged to participate. Many generations of natives and visitors to Livingston will never forget the sight of masked figures carrying lighted torches winding their way through the town, celebrating a medieval custom.

Alabama's Iron Curtain

TRAVELING from Huntsville in north Alabama to Mobile in south Alabama today is usually a matter of a few hours, but one hundred years ago it sometimes required weeks. North and south Alabama are separated by a rocky area known as Alabama's hill country, and in the days before cars and good roads these mountains were treacherous obstructions. Today this hill country has become the center of Alabama's industrial development and the home of its largest city, Birmingham, but a hundred years ago the area might be termed an "iron curtain" between north and south Alabama.

In 1859 John Milner attempted to get the state legislature to help finance the building of the Alabama Central Railroad through the hill country, but he was laughed into silence. One state senator from Calhoun County summarized the typical thinking of many: "That country up there is so poor that a buzzard would have to carry provisions on his back or starve to death on his passage."

The hill country had its champions, however. Many of these were farmers interested in the fact that some of their

He mined the coal by diving for it underwater after it had been loosened by crowbars

land appeared to contain iron ore. One of the most enthu siastic of this group was Bayliss Grace of Jefferson County. In the 1830's Grace took a load of "red dye" rock to Bibb County for testing and hammering into bars. From small beginnings such as this came the Birmingham steel area, today's largest in the South. Today also, iron ore is mined on the same property that Bayliss Grace farmed so many years ago.

Another native of the hill country, David Hanby, realized that mineral wealth was buried beneath the rocky soil. Hanby first came into the area as a blacksmith with Jackson's army. When the Indian wars were over he returned to Alabama and settled along the banks of the Warrior River. There he discovered seams of coal. Hanby mined the coal by diving for it underwater after it had been loosened by crowbars. Each year in the late fall he took advantage of the rise in the water to float his barges loaded with coal down to Mobile via the Warrior, Tombigbee, and Mobile waterways. The first time that he tried to sell the coal in Mobile nobody knew how to use it, and he had to go from door to door showing the people how to make a fire. Soon he had regular customers who waited the arrival of his coal barges each year.

The trip on the coal barges was hazardous, particularly at the Squaw Shoals above Tuscaloosa. In 1843 five out of twelve boats that Hanby had sent to Mobile were overturned at the Shoals. The men barely escaped with their lives and the cargo was lost. One of the most skillful riverboat pilots was Hanby's son, Felix, who had many trips to his credit.

Felix knew the course the awkward flatboats must take, and he could skillfully maneuver the fleet through the swirling waters of the Shoals. Today coal is still sent in barges from Birmingport to Mobile, but Lock 17 has replaced the treacherous Squaw Shoals.

Other champions of the hill country were the travelers who noticed the outcroppings of coal and iron ore as they journeyed through. In the 1830's young Frank Gilmer, as he crossed over Red Mountain, was puzzled by the red dust on his horse's hoofs. Curious, he dismounted, examined the purplish rocks, and slipped specimens into his saddlebag. He never forgot the iron ore buried in the hill country and many years later gave his financial support to the founding of Birmingham.

Of real importance to the development of the mineral belt was the 1850 report of Michael Tuomey, the state's first geologist. Tuomey explored the hill country with pick and hammer, discovering many of the coal and ore seams that were not developed until Birmingham was founded twenty years later. As a result of Tuomey's report, geologists came from all over the world to marvel at the unusual concentration of mineral deposits. When the first ton of iron was produced in the new city of Birmingham, Alabama's hill country had at last come into its own.

"The Man And The Hour Have Met"

SOMETIMES at the beginning of war, and always at its successful conclusion, people are overcome with enthusiasm and joy. When Alabama withdrew from the Union, a step toward war, there was general celebration throughout most of the state. Large crowds gathered at Montgomery to applaud the news that the South was seceding from the Union. People rushed to the lobbies, galleries, and floor of the Convention Chamber. Outside on the Capitol lawn, cannons boomed and banners began to fly majestically throughout the city. An immense flag of Alabama, presented in the name of the state's "patriotic ladies," was unfurled in the Convention Hall. Throughout the day the roar of celebrating guns continued. Henry C. Semple of Montgomery, who later became a Confederate soldier, made himself conspicuous by keeping his house in darkness when the houses of his neighbors were aflame with lighted candles in celebration of the adoption of the ordinance of secession. He remarked that the other houses on his street would be in mourning before the end of twelve months.

However, there was considerable disappointment in north Alabama because the ordinance of secession had not been referred to a popular vote. It was rumored that the United States flag continued to fly over the courthouse at Athens and Huntsville after adoption of secession. H. L. Clay, fearing rebellion in north Alabama and civil war in the state, said, "The state of Nickajack, to be formed by the counties of north Alabama and possibly by adjacent counties of Georgia and eastern Tennessee, looms grandly in the future in the imaginations of some of the leaders of the Union Party." But the feeling soon died, and people in north Alabama and south Alabama took up the tasks of organizing a confederate government for the seceded states by calling the Southern states to meet in Alabama in convention.

At the appointed time, February 4, 1861, delegates from all seceded states assembled in the Capitol at Montgomery and organized the Confederate States of America. Within four days a provisional constitution was adopted, and on the fifth day the convention elected Jefferson Davis as president and Alexander H. Stephens as vice-president. For the two top positions the Confederacy had selected recognized conservatives, men who had shown reluctance to secede. Jefferson Davis had long urged delay. Alexander H. Stephens had opposed secession until it was a fact. These two men had one other idea in common besides their hesitancy to leave the Union: they believed the North would use force to keep the Southern states from seceding.

Jefferson Davis, the president-elect, had to board a train in Meridian, Mississippi, to travel northeast to Chattanooga, Tennessee, then to Atlanta, Georgia, and back south to Montgomery. En route he made twenty-five speeches to

The clock struck one.   Jefferson Davis received the oath of office

crowds waiting with cheers, torches, and bonfires. Since there were no Pullman cars in those days, a bed had been set up for him in one of the coaches, but he had to rest fully dressed so that he could respond all through the night to the crowds that gathered at the stations to see and hear him.

The last crowd to meet him before his inauguration was on the balcony of the Exchange Hotel in Montgomery, where William L. Yancey as chief of the reception committee presented him with words that have now become famous: "The man and the hour have met."

On Monday, February 18, 1861, a new nation was born in the cradle of the Confederacy. Celebration of the event began early in the day. By midmorning a large crowd had gathered around the Capitol. Then shortly before noon the parade began along Dexter Avenue. First came the band, followed by the rhythmic marching of the First Alabama Regiment, and then a carriage, drawn by four white horses, bringing President-elect Jefferson Davis, Vice-President-elect Alexander Stephens, a minister, and an army officer. As Herman Arnold led his band up the avenue, his musicians began a tune never played before by a band anywhere. The tune was "Dixie," orchestrated only a week before by Arnold himself. On this first occasion it was called "I Wish I Was In Dixie's Land," the title under which it was published the preceding June as sheet music arranged for piano. When Arnold, a naturalized German musician who married a Montgomery girl, had asked his wife for help in selecting something new and exciting to play for the inauguration, she had suggested "Dixie." "Dixie" was a tune admirably

111

fitted to bring a sprawling young Confederacy together. The music was stirring, the soldiers marched briskly, the horses pranced. As Mr. Davis' carriage passed, the crowd cheered and fell in behind the procession in its progress up the street toward the crowded Capitol area.

The carriage arrived. The clock struck one. Howell Cobb administered the simple oath of office to Mr. Davis, who in turn made a brief inaugural speech. For the first and last time in its history, the South had installed a president of its own.

Free State Of Winston

WHILE the bands played "Dixie" and Jefferson Davis rode up Dexter Avenue in Montgomery, Alabama, to be inaugurated as President of the Confederate States of America, a different tune was being played in some parts of north Alabama. Secession was definitely an achievement of the large slave-holding planters, and these were more numerous in south Alabama than north Alabama. In north Alabama there was an independent-minded group of "mountain whites" struggling to make a living from their small rocky farms. These mountain people, rugged individuals who disliked the wealthy slave owners, opposed secession from the beginning and later ignored the Confederate civilian and military laws.

Even before war was declared, there was talk of withdrawing some of the northern counties from Alabama and joining these with some counties of east Tennessee. This gathering of counties would be called a new state named Nickajack. To some people in north Alabama, the coming of the Civil War made a new state of Nickajack even more desirable. Why should they fight the United States simply because Southern planters desired to secede from the Union?

113

A group of prominent citizens of Winston County in north Alabama planned a Fourth of July rally at Looney's Tavern in Houston to protest Alabama's secession from the Union. To advertise the meeting, riders went into the surrounding counties of Lawrence, Blount, Marshall, Walker, Fayette, Marion, and Franklin. As a result, twenty-five hundred people attended the meeting, yelling support of resolutions which questioned the right of Alabama to secede from the Union. With United States flags waving over their heads, speakers affirmed the right of north Alabama counties to remain neutral. The flag waving was too much for one of the few Confederate sympathizers present. Making fun of the fact that Winston was only one county in the whole state of Alabama, he shouted from the back of the crowd, "Winston secedes. Hurray for the 'free state of Winston.'" Today people still refer to the free state of Winston.

When the Confederate government tried to enforce its conscription laws and jailed the men who resisted, some of the people in north Alabama, now called Tories or "neutralists," became actively hostile to the state of Alabama. They formed guerilla bands, hiding in mountain strongholds and sweeping into the neighboring fertile valleys to rob and pillage.

When General Buell of the Union Army occupied parts of north Alabama in April, 1862, several thousand citizens with no devotion to the Confederate cause rallied around him for help and comfort. It was estimated that as many as ten thousand men sought refuge in the mountains of north Alabama during the Civil War. Some of these were

114

With United States flags waving, speakers affirmed the right of north Alabama counties to remain neutral

deserters from the Confederate Army, and some were Tories or "neutralists" from Alabama and Tennessee, men who had refused to help the South fight the North.

A few people in north Alabama not only refused to fight the Union, they themselves joined the Union armies and fought the South. However, these numbers were small; official records show that only 2,678 Alabama white men actually enlisted in the United States Army. Of these 2,678, 2,066 saw service in the First Alabama Cavalry, the only white Union regiment from the state. The revolt of the "Tories of the Hill" is an unusual chapter in Alabama history, important today because it throws light on the many different sections of Alabama's population.

Making Salt In Alabama

A glance at Alabama's saltworks during the Civil War gives a "bird's eye view" of the problems at home in Alabama. As in all wars, while the soldiers are suffering at the front, the population at home suffers from scarcity of items and from profiteering by people making "war profits." One of many scarce items in the South during the war was salt, and a most important salt supply was the saltworks in Clarke, Washington, and Mobile Counties in Alabama.

Though it takes good imagination to picture it, there were approximately two thousand people at one time during the war helping to make salt in the area of Jackson in Clarke County, with lesser numbers in other salt areas in south Alabama. The many wagons and horses and pedestrians in and out of the Jackson area suggested the activity of a carnival, or fair, or perhaps huge ball game. Entire families accompanied by their slaves came to the area of Jackson and pitched camp so that they could make enough salt to take home for a winter's use. Center of the saltworks area was Salt Mountain, an almost perpendicular hill six miles south of Jackson, a landmark that can be seen today.

Saltmaking is easy in large areas of south Alabama. All that is needed is a well deep enough to reach the salt water or brine, then a kettle in which to boil away the water so that only salt remains, and finally a fire for heating the kettle. It was the same in Alabama a hundred years ago. Of course some of the wells had to go down as far as one hundred feet, but in lower swamps a number of wells found brine after a half dozen or so feet. Getting the brine up was similar to getting water from ordinary wells: by using a rope, bucket, and pulley. The bucketfuls of brine were tossed into the large kettles, more pine wood was fed to the fire under the kettle, and the water was boiled until only the salt remained. Seven or eight kettles of brine would produce one kettle of salt. At the beginning of the war, small kettles and crude fireplaces were seen across the more than three thousand acres of salt lands being "farmed" in south Alabama.

As war progressed, and both the federal government and private industry became interested, large furnaces made of brick began to heat large kettles over the salt lands. This was little reminiscent of a century or so earlier when Indians observed that animals returned again and again to the area to lap at small springs or pools, subsequently named "salt springs." The salt season in south Alabama during the war extended mainly from April to December because in the other months the rivers overflowed, submerging the salt lands and preventing work. Even after the water drained away, the seepage of fresh water into the wells was sometimes too great to permit saltmaking.

In 1861 salt was selling at the saltworks at $1.25 per

An "inexhaustible quantity" of brine and salt was in Clarke County,
Alabama

119

bushel of fifty pounds, and this price increased almost daily. Alabama Governor A. B. Moore called such profiteering at the saltworks with its commodity so necessary to the Confederate cause, "unpatriotic and wicked." He began to recommend to the state legislature that it pass laws to supervise the salt business in Alabama. The Confederacy required six million bushels or three hundred million pounds of salt a year. When the blockade shut off the usual sources of supply early in the Civil War, salt was indeed critical to the support of the South. So Governor Moore's anxiety was understandable, especially since some of the so-called salt springs were on state-owned property, and the state was having as much difficulty in supervising its own salt production as that of private individuals. Yet Governor Moore's anxiety was somewhat allayed when he learned that by the winter of 1862 salt workers on private property and on state property in Clarke and Washington counties were producing over two thousand bushels of salt a day. The governor's anxiety was relieved in this regard, but it increased when he thought of salt prices. The state could control the price of salt on its land, but profiteers began to see the advantage of the much greater salt potential on privately owned property, and prices began to leap.

By late 1862 salt was selling for four dollars and more a bushel. During 1863 it rose from fifteen to twenty to thirty dollars a bushel. During 1864 it rose from thirty to forty dollars and finally was selling at the unbelievable price of fifty dollars a bushel by the end of the war. Citizens were of course angry at having to pay such a price. But many Confederate people found it necessary to do so.

Yes, the south Alabama saltworks was one of the most famous new enterprises in the Confederacy during the war. Although northern Alabama counties bought their salt from Virginia because of a more reasonable price and cheaper transportation costs, many thousands of people in the deep South depended on Alabama for their salt. Governor Pettus of Mississippi announced that an "inexhaustible quantity" of brine and salt was in Clarke County, Alabama, and Mississippi established its own salt manufacturing company in the county.

The south Alabama saltworks thrived despite unhealthy living conditions that made some families afraid to go to the area or risk sending their slaves. Helping none to improve the area's reputation was a smallpox epidemic which left a large cemetery on a hill in the saltworks area, a cemetery that can be seen today.

The war itself also came to the saltworks. There was the fear throughout the war that Union troops might raid the area and destroy the works. A logical way to have done this would have been Federal boats up the Tombigbee River. To forestall this, the Confederacy erected a battery of guns at Carney's Bluff and another battery at Oven Bluff, and other fortifications at Choctaw Bluff. These fortifications were intended to protect not only the saltworks, but also to protect shipbuilding operations where gunboats were being constructed on a level plain near Oven Bluff. There was in addition a navy yard on the Tombigbee River in Clarke County near Sunflower Bend. But the only Union attack in the area was apparently by a single gunboat that was said

As the war ended, so did the making of salt in Alabama

to have steamed up from Mobile to Gosport in Clarke County and to have destroyed a warehouse there. Probably the reason this boat passed Choctaw Bluff unharmed was that the trip was made at the time of very low waters, and the muzzles of the cannons on the bluff could not be lowered sufficiently to fire at the boat.

Besides its reputation for unhealthy living conditions and the likelihood of Union raids, the saltworks also had a reputation for bad local citizenry in the area. A Mr. A. J. Cawley was forced by angry salt workers to leave the area for selling whiskey to slaves and receiving stolen salt in return. At about this time also, the CLARKE COUNTY DEMOCRAT estimated that there were "90 or 100" deserters from the Confederate Army among the people manufacturing salt. Because of overall conditions, the laborers at the works were mostly slaves pressed into service. But even a number of these slaves earned the reputation for burning fences, damaging wells, taking ropes off buckets, and stealing any food in the area that wasn't watched with care. Because of the reputation for lawlessness around the saltworks during the war, the CLARKE COUNTY DEMOCRAT announced with pleasure near the beginning of 1863 that the Alabama Methodist Conference had appointed a preacher for the saltworks circuit.

As the war ended, so did the making of salt in south Alabama. In 1865 Clarke County disposed of "a number of mules, oxen, wagons, and other property which was used at the County Salt Works during the war," the items to be "sold at public auction to the highest bidder." The state of Mississippi also had to dispose of "several salt wells, furnaces, and 480 acres of timberland at the Alabama salt wells, with a large array of work shops, cabins, offices, sheds, tanks and other equipment."

Today the salt springs in Alabama still flow, but barring a second war, or other emergency, people in the area will probably never discontinue buying their salt at the nearest grocery store.

The Ladies Who Faced Federal Troops

EARLY in the Civil War, when Union troops prepared to attack her college, Madame J. Hamilton Childs saw to it that not even a tree was harmed. In the spring of 1862 the entire Athens College student body of thirty-two girls went into near panic at sight of enemy soldiers on the front lawn, but college president Madame Childs was determined that school would not be interrupted. A lady with a stature as stately as the columns of the school's famous Founders Hall at Athens, Alabama, she put on her white lace cap, opened the door and strode firmly down the walk toward the soldiers, her black skirts swirling with the dignified air of a perfect Southern lady.

"I want to speak to the officer in charge," she said with an authoritative voice that echoed to every "blue coat" present.

The officer marched forward. "We have orders to raze the college, Ma'am," he said.

Madame Childs didn't say a word as she dug down into the folds of her dress for a paper which she handed to the officer. He read it, paused, and handed it back. Then the girls inside the building, whose faces had been glued to the window panes ever since their president and idol had stepped outside, witnessed an unusual scene.

The officer snapped to attention, smartly saluted Madame Childs as she stood proudly erect. Then he turned to his soldiers. "Set up a battery here," he ordered. "No one will be permitted to harm this school."

Madame Childs returned inside, and the education of the thirty-two girls continued without further interruption. No damage was done to the building. It was the only Methodist college in the South to survive the horrors of war intact.

For many years, until twenty-five years ago in fact, when the last "girl" died at age ninety-three, the story of that fateful morning was told in the region around Athens by graduates of the school who were present when Madame Childs presented her letter to the Union captain. And every girl, without exception, always declared that the principal had said: "I HAD A LETTER FROM ABRAHAM LINCOLN."

Like Madame Childs, another Alabama lady also faced Federal troops on a campus of higher learning. Mrs. L. C. Garland, wife of the president of the University of Alabama, braved a fiery death in confronting Union troops. In April, 1865, the Union general, John T. Croxton, led his troops to attack the University of Alabama. On that night the young students who must defend the University were asleep in their dormitories. Dr. Peter Bryce, Supervisor of Bryce Hospital adjoining the University campus, sounded the

As stately in stature as Founders Hall, Madame Childs put on her white lace cap

127

alarm. At about 12:30 Dr. L. C. Garland, University president, started hurrying across the campus. "Tell them to beat the long roll, the Yanks are in town." The University's drum corpsmen sounded their drums, and sleepy cadets leaped from their beds to uphold the honor of the university and Tuscaloosa. In less than five minutes the first company had formed, as cadets and professors assumed fighting military formations and began hurrying down the road at "double time" to face the "Feds" before they could reach the campus.

However, the cadets and professors were too late. The Federals, far outnumbering the defenders, had already seized the Confederate artillery housed in the livery stable. The battle was over by one o'clock. The Federals had captured sixty prisoners and in turn had suffered twenty-three casualties. Only one Confederate had been wounded, and that wound was not fatal.

The men of Croxton's command began destroying the university which had given such valued service to the Confederate cause. Almost all of the buildings went up in flames, and some of the professors' homes were threatened. The explosion of powder, captured by the Federals, could be heard for miles around Tuscaloosa.

The professor in charge of the university library, one of the finest libraries in the South, made a brave attempt to save it. He appealed to the officer in charge of the raiding squad. This officer must have appreciated books, for he restrained his men while he asked General Croxton whether the library might be spared. The general explained curtly that his orders demanded that the library be burned. The

While the library burned, Mrs. Garland began the defense of her home

129

officer then entered the library, selected for himself a rare and valuable copy of the KORAN, and then ordered the building burned to the ground. It was a dry season and the flames spread at once.

While the library burned in plain view of her own front porch, Mrs. Garland began the defense of her home. With Dr. Garland away in the company of his ill-fated cadets, Mrs. Garland had no one to protect her but her servants at the president's mansion. The soldiers piled furniture in the center of the building and set fire to the beautiful structure. As fast as the flames caught, Mrs. Garland and her servants stamped them out.

The officer at the scene could not long face the determination of this Alabama lady. He ordered his men to put out the fires and replace the furniture and then, with admiration, he earnestly assured her that she would be molested no further.

These two Alabama women helped to preserve, in whole or in part, buildings of higher learning which stand today as monuments to Alabama history.

Little Grand Canyon

DURING the Civil War, with the Confederates close behind him, General Andrew May was pushing his troops through northeast Alabama trying to join Sherman's army in Georgia. Suddenly a Union scout reined his horse to an abrupt stop before the general, and reported, "There's a hole as big as all outdoors up ahead, sir, and I can't find a way around it."

General May and his staff rushed forward to see for themselves. The general walked cautiously to the edge of the "hole" and his eyes widened in astonishment as he looked down into a tremendous gorge.

"This is unbelievable," he shouted to an officer standing carefully behind him. "Here we are on top of Lookout Mountain, and there is a gully here that looks like a little Grand Canyon."

Trapped on the edge of the canyon, the Federals were routed by the Confederates, but General May escaped. He could not forget the natural wonder that he had seen hidden in the forests of north Alabama, and after the war he came back to make a survey of the canyon. He discovered that

General May walked cautiously to the edge of the "hole"

the chasm was the deepest and largest east of the Rockies, being seven hundred feet deep and twelve miles around its rim. Just as the Colorado River had cut the Grand Canyon so had Little River chiseled out this canyon with its narrow rushing waters in the gorge. On the tall cliffs bordering the canyon, General May explored the remains of ancient Indian cave shelters.

Tracing the canyon to its source, General May found it to be DeSoto Falls, tumbling 120 feet into Little River. Just below the falls a massive ledge of jutting rock opened into a natural cave with several rooms which had been enlarged and connected by the Indians. Legend says that Hernando DeSoto had raided these caves looking for gold in 1540.

When General May finished his survey, he wrote across the bottom of his report, "May's Gulf." This unusual spot was known by that name until 1954 when it became a part of DeSoto State Park. At the dedication ceremonies at Eberhart Point in August, 1954, May's Gulf became officially Little River Canyon.

Fiercest Naval Battle Of The Civil War

"FULL steam ahead," ordered Admiral David Farragut of the Union Navy. With these words he led the Union Navy into Mobile Bay, and the fiercest naval battle of the Civil War was underway, August 5, 1864. The torpedoes in question had been laid under water by the Confederates in an attempt to protect Mobile Bay and the four ships of their Navy anchored there.

Farragut, with seventeen ships under his command, expected to make short work of the TENNESSEE, sister ship to the ironclad MERRIMAC, and the three gunboats. First he must pass the guns of Fort Morgan guarding the entrance to the Bay. Noting that the wind was from the west, he threw a screen between his ship and the gunners at the fort by igniting gunpowder on the ship's deck, and the smoke was carried to the fort. No sooner had he passed the fort, however, than the lead ship, the TECUMSEH, struck a torpedo and immediately sank, but the rest of the fleet passed safely through the line.

After the guns of Fort Morgan had failed to turn back the enemy, the TENNESSEE and the three little gunboats

He led the Union Navy into Mobile Bay, and the fiercest naval battle of the Civil War was underway

135

came forth to defend themselves and the city. Within a
short time all three gunboats were knocked out of battle,
but the lone ship TENNESSEE fought on. For four hours
she matched her six guns and two hundred men against
seventeen ships, 199 guns, seven hundred men, and one of
the greatest admirals of all times. Confederate Admiral
Buchanan, who had sworn never to surrender, rammed ship
after ship. Finally with her steering gear shot away the
TENNESSEE surrendered but not until Admiral Buchanan
had been knocked out by his own men so that the next in
command could surrender.

Birmingham Is Born

WHILE "carpetbaggers" and "scalawags" were busy seeking personal gain during the Reconstruction in Alabama, an opposing group of loyal natives were just as busy enticing Northern capitalists to develop Alabama's mineral resources. In the late 1860's these loyal Alabamians used methods to attract industry that one finds familiar today. They advertised in Northern newspapers and magazines, inviting interested parties to make "an all expense-paid trip" and see for themselves the fabulous mineral belt of Alabama.

In 1869 some of these farsighted Alabama men met in Montgomery and formed the Elyton Land Company for the purpose of building in Jefferson County a mining town to be located where the railroads, then under construction, would cross. The first job of the new company was to select a leader. What they needed was a promoter, a man with brains, imagination, and money who could put the new town on the map. The man they wanted for the job was the wealthy and influential James R. Powell, former resident of Montgomery but then living on his Mississippi plantation.

When Powell was informed of the plans, he sent experts to examine the resources around Jefferson County. Their report convinced him that this was a scheme "worth his mettle, worth his time and worth his money, indeed something with millions in it." So when he was elected president of the Elyton Land Company in 1871, James R. Powell accepted.

In electing James R. Powell as president of the Elyton Land Company, the founders of the company hoped that Powell's "rags to riches" personal history would be repeated in the history of this new land company. They remembered that Powell, aged nineteen, had ridden into Alabama in 1833 to seek his fortune, his worldly possessions consisting of the mare which he rode and twenty dollars concealed in his money belt. Powell's first job had been as a pony express rider carrying the mail from Montgomery to Nashville. When the government abolished the pony express, authorizing mail to be carried by stagecoach, Powell, who already had showed a sharp business sense, was ready for it. He had saved enough money to buy a few wagons, and these he now covered with cloth, starting his own stagecoach line, carrying passengers as well as mail through central and northern Alabama.

Soon Powell expanded his business ventures to include the operation of hotels in Montgomery and Lowndesboro and the buying of cotton lands in Mississippi. He was elected to the State Legislature, but after serving two terms he left politics to devote his full time to his stagecoach business, now threatened by a rival line operated by Robert Jemison of Tuscaloosa. The two men started a cut-rate war that was about to bankrupt both of them. Finally, to save themselves they were forced to consolidate, and the *Jemison, Powell, Ficklen and Company Stage Coach Line* was organized.

Powell had foreseen the Civil War and had taken steps to protect his fortune and his family during the war period. He invested much of his fortune in foreign markets, and he sent his wife and daughter to live in Europe. Being too old to serve as a soldier, he gave his time and money to the Confederacy by outfitting companies and obtaining supplies.

Within a short time after Powell was elected president of the Elyton Land Company, he arrived in Jones Valley with John Milner to lay out the town. Milner, who had first seen Jefferson County when he was surveying for the South and North Railroad, had dreamed for years of founding a mining town in the area. Now it would be done. The two men stood in front of the section houses of the railroad, the only buildings besides a blacksmith's shop, and looked out across a few corn fields. The rest of the land was a low flat marsh covered with water and a jungle of vines and trees.

"This is it," Milner said. "Not much to look at now but the wealth is here—in Red Mountain and the coal fields. We may live to see this the coal and iron center of the world."

"We'll make it that, "Powell replied. "We'll advertise this town from Mobile to New York. I'll get the people here. It will be your job to see that they get coal and iron ore out of the hills."

"Fair enough," Milner answered. "I've arranged with the

139

railroad company for the Elyton Land people to stay in one of the section houses. We'll all eat together in the log cabin in the back. No doubt we'll 'have coal dust in the gravy and iron ore in the soup,' but it will be better than lodgings in Elyton. My cousin has sent horses over for us to use so let's take a look around now."

For the next three days the two men covered every foot of the land owned by the Elyton Land Company in Jones Valley. They agreed on the location of schools, churches, and parks. The streets were to be laid out on a checkerboard pattern. Then they consulted with Major William P. Barker, the civil engineer, who was in charge of the work. The leveling of the ground and stacking of the lots began. Soon work had progressed far enough for Powell to announce that a public auction of lots would be held June 1, 1871.

Even though Birmingham would not be chartered for another six months, word of the auction had gotten around, and at daybreak on June 1, 1871, people started arriving. They came in wagons, on horseback, in buggies, and on foot. When the crowd had become large enough, Powell mounted the auctioneer's block. He told the people about the great mineral deposits in Red Mountain; about the nearby coal fields of Warrior, Coosa, and Cahaba; about the railroad which would soon be ready to carry Birmingham products to eager markets. "Never before in the history of the world have such valuable minerals been found so close to each other," Powell told the crowd. "This is your chance to make millions."

The auctioneer then took the stand, and Lot Number

One at First Avenue and Nineteenth Street was up for sale.

"What am I bid, ladies and gentlemen, for this choice business site?" the auctioneer said.

"Fifty dollars," spoke up a farmer from Shelby County.

"One hundred and fifty dollars," said Major Andrew Marre.

"One hundred and fifty dollars—one time, two time, three time," the auctioneer said. "Sold."

When the corner lot at First Avenue and Twentieth Street was put up, a man with a foreign accent spoke immediately and bought the lot for four hundred dollars.

"That's Captain Charles Linn from Montgomery," somebody said. "He's a Swedish sea captain; crossed the Atlantic sixty-five times, they say. He landed in Montgomery as a deck hand on a river boat in the 'forties. He decided to settle there, and he made a fortune in the mercantile business."

"What are you going to do with that lot, Captain?" Powell shouted through the crowd.

"Build a bank, Colonel Powell, as you well know," the captain replied, shaking his finger at Powell accusingly.

"Now what did he mean by that?" somebody asked.

"The captain was a friend of Powell's in Montgomery, and Powell sold him on the idea of building a bank by sending him a model, on which was inscribed 'The National Bank of Birmingham, Charles Linn, President.' "

Another corner lot at First Avenue and Twentieth Street was sold for one hundred and fifty dollars to Benjamin P. Worthington, a cotton planter of Jones Valley.

After the auction, the corn fields began to disappear as

141

*Powell spent his time now talking to every stranger that came to
inspect the new town*

142

if by magic; construction started in earnest. Two brick companies, one from Montgomery, the other from Coosa County, agreed to come to Birmingham and make, on the spot, one million brick each. Powell guaranteed the companies that their bricks would be bought as fast as they were made. To assure this, he had the Elyton Land Company order that all buildings in the business district must be made of brick, must be at least two stories high, and must be built within twelve months after the purchase of the lot.

Powell spent his time now talking to every stranger that came to inspect the new town. He took him on a tour of the coal and iron land of the company, and over the business district. "Why, within three weeks time," he would say, "a man can buy a lot, build a store and start making money."

Powell knew people all over the state, and he traveled to every part of it, telling his friends of the opportunities in Birmingham and inviting them to come see for themselves. Many of them came, and Powell soon discovered that the town needed a hotel to accommodate everyone. He quickly built an Elyton Land Company hotel called the Relay House, and got his friends from Rome, Georgia, Mr. and Mrs. William Ketchum, to run it.

"I want the Relay House to be the Birmingham home of my friends," Powell said to Mrs. Ketchum as they looked over the beautifully furnished parlors, just completed. "You can help me attract here the type of men that will build a town—not those gadflies who come in on one train and go out on the next looking for an easy dollar. Saloons and

143

gambling houses are springing up along First Avenue faster than I can count them."

"Why don't we open the Relay House with a party, Colonel Powell? You can invite your friends to see the kind of establishment we are running," Mrs. Ketchum suggested. "Besides it's time this town had some social life. Everyone is working too hard."

The party was a great success. Guests declared they had never seen more elegant furnishings, or tasted better refreshments. For every girl there were five to ten young men. Powell had a great time greeting old friends and showing them around the rooms.

"Did you notice the tall gilt-frame mirrors?" Powell asked a group in one of the parlors. "They came from the White House of the Confederacy. Jeff Davis stood in front of one of them and took a last look at himself before going to his inauguration."

"Mighty interesting, sir," said a young man standing close to Powell. "When are you going to move the state capital up to Birmingham?"

Powell and the group laughed loudly at this remark, and he replied, "We have Capitol Park ready."

Powell had prophesied that the population of Birmingham would be quadrupled within a year. In his report to the Elyton Land Company stockholders for 1872, he stated that Birmingham now had a population of four thousand as compared to nine hundred the year before. There were five hundred houses, fifty-four brick buildings, six churches, four hotels, and one playhouse. In January, 1873, Powell

144

was elected mayor, and from then on people called him "The Duke of Birmingham."

Powell liked to ride his horse to the top of Red Mountain to get a good look at "his town." It made him proud to see the buildings along First Avenue and the houses up and down Fifth and Sixth Avenue. Even the tents pitched along Village Creek looked good to him because they were occupied by families waiting for houses to be completed. He could almost see the shafts of John Milner's mine at Newcastle which was producing seventy tons of coal a day. When he turned around he could look into Shades Valley and see smoke rising from the Oxmoor furnaces. He remembered what the New York Press Association members had said about Birmingham after holding their 1873 meeting here. They had written that "Birmingham is destined to be the manufacturing center of the habitable globe."

"Just two years ago," Powell said to himself, "those men could have stood here and seen only farms and marshes. We have come a long way." Several months later in June of 1873 Powell sat at his desk writing an article about Birmingham for a New York paper. He was interrupted when a messenger hurried into his office. "I've come from Dr. Jordan, sir," the messenger announced. "He said to tell you that cholera has broken out."

Powell leaped to his feet. "I can't believe it," he said. "It will ruin the town."

"I'm afraid it is true, sir. Dr. Jordan said for you to come to his office at once."

The cholera spread into epidemic size overnight, and the

Henry DeBardeleben and John Milner foresaw the red glow that lights up the night sky of Birmingham as the furnaces go about their business of making steel

crowded trains that had brought people into Birmingham were now overloaded with people fleeing the dreaded disease. Stores closed, and the loudest sound on the once busy streets was the rumble of the hearse.

At last the cholera epidemic was over, and for the first time in many weeks Powell returned to his office. As he sat at his desk, his eye fell on the article he had been writing when news came concerning the cholera. He read: "Never has there been a locality where all the raw materials for the manufacture of iron . . . can be found in such. . ." It seemed to Powell years since he had written these words, yet it had been only a few weeks. He dropped the paper into the trash can and walked over to the window to look up at Red Mountain.

"Birmingham will come back," he said to himself, "for the iron ore and the coal are stronger than any of us. But I can't do it again."

Powell turned again to his desk and picked up a report from the Elyton Land Company. He saw that the company's stock was down to one half of its original value. With the company in bankruptcy there would be no hope, for it was the backbone of the town. He dipped his pen in ink and wrote: "To the stockholders of the Elyton Land Company. I hereby tender my resignation as president of the Elyton Land Company. . . ."

But the company persuaded Powell to stay on, and it was not until 1875 that he settled all of his business in Birmingham and left for his Mississippi plantation.

Birmingham did come back after several years. The work

of Powell was carried on by other men such as Henry De-Bardeleben and John Milner, who foresaw the red glow that lights up the night sky of Birmingham today as the furnaces go about their business of making steel.

Atop Red Mountain stands the statue of Vulcan, symbol of Birmingham's industrial might. Standing fifty-five feet high and weighing 120,000 pounds, Vulcan is America's second largest statue, next to the Statue of Liberty. Vulcan is an appropriate monument to Birmingham's industrial pioneers, beginning with Powell, DeBardeleben, and Milner and reflecting upon their descendents, some of whom are Birmingham's farsighted pioneers of today.

From Cotton To Steel

WHEN the first furnace in the infant city of Birmingham was "blown in," there was no doubt in anybody's mind as to who was responsible. Her owner and builder, Henry DeBardeleben, was himself as tall and dark and distinguished as the furnace he had built. Neither was there doubt that he had named the furnace after his oldest daughter, Alice, for it was the custom of the day.

That cold November day in 1880 when Alice was "blown in" was a gala occasion. On the successful operation of this furnace depended the future of Birmingham and of industrial Alabama. Since its founding only nine years before, Birmingham had struggled to stay alive. There was more talk of what the Birmingham district could do than action, but the energetic and resourceful DeBardeleben set about to change that. With the help of T. T. Hillman, who had grown up in the furnace business, he organized the Alice Furnace Company and started construction. Soon the seventy-five-foot stack of Alice was the most discernible landmark of the young town.

A large crowd had gathered to witness the "blowing in"

Birmingham entered upon a boom period, for pig iron could be made by using Alabama coal and ore

of the first blast furnace in Birmingham. Special trains ran for the occasion and refreshments were served. The handsome DeBardeleben was prominent in the crowd, greeting old friends and joshing with his rivals. "Why, I bet she'll do fifty tons a day," he declared. Everyone knew that De-Bardeleben had successfully rebuilt the Oxmoor furnace after the Civil War and that he had done a good job of running his father-in-law's cotton gin, but just what he knew about a blast furnace remained to be seen.

It didn't take Alice long to start producing those fifty tons a day. Birmingham entered upon a boom period, for Alice had at last proved that pig iron could be made by using Alabama coal and ore. Frequently the night skies glowed red as the busy furnace put forth its pigs. Orders from steel plants all over the country poured in, and Birmingham boomed.

With his faith in Birmingham proved but his health impaired, DeBardeleben sold his interest in the Birmingham district for one million dollars. He was living then in a little two-room cabin, one room of which was his office. In these unpretentious surroundings the papers were signed closing the first million dollar deal in the Alabama coal and iron trade. It was more than appropriate that Birmingham's famous adventurer, DeBardeleben, should reap such a reward.

The James Brothers And
The Muscle Shoals Robbery

FRANK AND JESSE JAMES enjoyed their stay at the St. James Hotel in Selma. The manager said they behaved like perfect gentlemen, and he spent a large part of the day playing billiards with them in the hotel's billiard room. He enjoyed playing with them, but it was only because he did not know that his guests were the famous James brothers, leaders of an outlaw band, wanted by the law. He did think it a little odd that the brothers, who called themselves "Williams," wanted separate rooms. He found out later they used separate rooms so that if one was captured, the other could free him.

The James brothers were in Selma on a peaceful mission in March of 1881. They had come to visit their boyhood playmate and fellow soldier in the Confederate Army, John Green Norris. In order not to embarrass the Norris family nor implicate Norris himself with the law, the James brothers visited with him only at night in his home behind locked doors. When the brothers left Selma, no one was poorer for it. But when they got to Muscle Shoals, Alabama, on their

152

way back to their farms in Tennessee, it was a different story.

Alexander G. Smith, paymaster for the United States Army, was riding along Muscle Shoals Canal two miles from Florence with $5,200.00 in his saddle bags, the payroll for the engineers' camp at Bluewater. That was at 4:00 p.m. on March 11, 1881. By 4:10 Mr. Smith had been disarmed, tied up and robbed by three masked horsemen with pistols. According to historians, responsibility for the robbery rested on none other than the "world's most notorious desperadoes," the James gang.

It was not until 1884 that the authorities in Alabama got around to doing something about the Muscle Shoals robbery. In the meantime, just one month after the robbery, Jesse James had been shot in the back and killed by a member of his own gang. "Wild Bill" Ryan, who had accompanied the James brothers in the Muscle Shoals robbery, was serving a twenty-five-year prison sentence. Only Frank James was left available for trial.

The trial of Frank James in Huntsville was one of the most exciting events in that city's history. It was a lean and calculating prisoner who entered the courtroom in 1884. For two months he had undergone the stares of hundreds of curiosity seekers outside his filthy cell in Huntsville's jail. For two months he had been no more than a caged animal on display for everyone to see. True, he had played the part, attempting to please the crowds that passed his cell during the two months. He had kept his mustache trimmed and had puffed his cigars rapidly. For good measure, he had read Shakespeare while the curious stared. He spoke gently with the ladies and smiled at more than one. If the bars

153

If the bars had not separated them, Frank James would have patted some of the children on the head

had not separated them, he would have patted some of the children on the head. To former Civil War soldiers like himself he turned many a neat phrase about the good old days when he like they protected the South. He invited the Huntsville press for interviews and told them they should be thankful to him for giving them something to write about. His disarming manner paid off, for the press was more than kind to him in their stories. The reporters began to find him surprisingly unlike any outlaw they could imagine. It would take some proving to get twelve men to believe that this man had robbed the paymaster at Muscle Shoals.

The legends of Frank and Jesse James had for many years made them famous. It required little persuasion now to win numerous people of Huntsville to Frank's side before the trial started. And persuasion was one thing Frank James had, whether in the form of quick thinking or quick triggering.

Yes, Frank James was determined never again to grace a Huntsville jail, that April in 1884 when he entered the court. The room was packed with out-of-state as well as local spectators. Accompanying Frank at the trial was his wife, Ann Ralton, and their six-year-old son, Robert Frank. It was said by some that son Frank resembled a little prince so neat was his attire. The father's clothes too were neat, his mustache trimmed, and his shoes shined. This was no craven prisoner, begging for mercy at whatever cost.

The government's star witness was James Andrew Liddell, one-time member of the James gang, now turning state's evidence so that the government would not prosecute him in turn. It was Liddell who had schemed with Bob and Charlie Ford to kill Jesse. Liddell claimed he had heard the James brothers and "Wild Bill" Ryan plotting the Alabama holdup. The jurors frowned. Such circumstantial evidence was coming from a witness who was a known murderer and horse stealer. One of Liddell's known recent murders had been especially gruesome. In December of 1881 he had put a bullet several inches "above the right eye" of Wood Hite, after having been accused of carrying on with Wood's young stepmother. The HUNTSVILLE DEMOCRAT said that Liddell was "unworthy of belief without satisfactory corroboration by creditable witnesses, and this was lacking."

Frank himself was the picture of fatherly innocence as he glanced now and then toward his wife and son. He also glanced toward his six witnesses who would swear that he could not have been at the scene of the crime. He was in Nashville at the time, they would say. To bolster the government's losing case, the prosecutor at one time asked the prisoner to put on a "slouch hat" and walk about the courtroom to see if this resemblance to a bandit might not jar the poor memories of reluctant government witnesses. The prisoner performed the feat with a "firm and steady eye, to and fro."

The jury appeared anything but confused when it retired shortly before six. It appeared even less confused when it returned soon afterwards. The foreman spoke without hesitation. "Not guilty as charged, Your Honor."

The crowd had sensed it coming. Hands were partly raised, ready to clap. Cheering echoed back and forth across the courtroom. On leaving the courtroom behind the rapidly moving Frank James, many an Alabamian expressed regret that Frank's itinerary called for him to return to Missouri the next day. But not so Frank. If he had regrets at leaving, he didn't express them.

In Missouri the famous outlaw became a model citizen. He lived for thirty years as shoe salesman, race track starter, farmer, and circus entertainer, in all capacities a well-liked and diplomatic man. Always a good conversationalist, he spoke now and then of his Huntsville trial. And years later, as his mind became hazy, it was suggested by some that Frank return to Huntsville, to jog his memory concerning the more salient points of his Huntsville trial. Frank disagreed. He and the Huntsville jail had parted friends many years before, and he saw no reason to change things now.

Everybody came to see the "airyplane"

Airplanes Come To Alabama

WHEN alert Fred S. Ball, President of the Montgomery Commercial Club in 1910, learned that Wilbur Wright was in town searching for a site on which to start a flying school, he wasted no time in appointing a committee to assist him. One of the committeemen was Frank D. Kohn, who jokingly told Wright about three hundred acres he owned that "were flat as the back of your hand and as unproductive as a volcano."

"Let's take a look at it," Wright said. "I've seen everything else and none of it will do."

After a careful look at Kohn's acres, he exclaimed, "Just what I want. I need room for a big field with few obstructions, and this is it."

Kohn gave him use of the land free, and Montgomery had taken its first step in championing the cause of aviation.

On March 26, 1910, Orville Wright piloted the first plane to be flown in Montgomery on the site selected by his brother. It was launched on a 192-foot monorail, built in sections so that it could be moved around the field as the wind changed. Wright had five pupils, and he announced that his daily jaunts were for instruction, not exhibition. To the people of Montgomery and the surrounding area, however, this was the best show the city had offered them since Jefferson Davis rode up Dexter Avenue to be inaugurated as President of the Confederacy. The railroads ran special trains and everybody came to see the "airyplane." The flights lasted only five minutes and didn't get much higher than the telephone poles, but that was enough for the citizens of 1910, many of whom still regarded a "horseless carriage" with suspicion.

The Wright brothers' school lasted only a few months, but Montgomery's interest in aviation had now been kindled. During World War I, John Kohn, brother of Fred, succeeded in getting the U. S. Army to locate a repair depot for nearby airfields on the same site used by the Wright brothers. Kohn sold the original five hundred acres to the U. S. Government, and a field was built in 1918 called the Montgomery Engine and Repair Depot. In 1922 the name was changed to Maxwell Field in honor of Lt. William C. Maxwell of Atmore, Alabama, who had crashed in the Philippines while serving with the Army Air Force. Today Maxwell Air Force Base lies in the center of the original tract.

Rooster Bridge

THE state of Alabama had barely started celebrating its one hundredth anniversary when it faced a crisis as great in its own way as any in the preceding century. The Dixie Overland Highway running 2880 miles from Savannah, Georgia, to San Diego, California, could not be completed in 1919 because there was no money to build a bridge across the Tombigbee River in Alabama. There was much consternation throughout the state as well as the nation. In fact, one Alabamian was so distraught at this seeming obstruction to travel across the state, he stood on the banks of the Tombigbee at Demopolis in 1919 and asked himself, "What will it take to get the people of Alabama to raise enough money for this bridge?" This Alabamian's name was Frank Derby, a man already known for his ability to get things done.

Derby had previously staged several cattle shows at the Tutwiler Hotel in Birmingham, where thousands of people had come to view a prize-winning white bull in the middle of the hotel lobby. As he looked across the Tombigbee River at Demopolis toward the Sumter County side, he remembered that Sumter was sometimes called the Game Cock County because it was named for General Sumter, the Revolutionary War hero, who was nicknamed "The Game Cock." That brought to Derby's mind the headline in every daily paper in 1919, the meeting of the Big Four in France. "Those Big Four are the gamecocks of today," Derby thought. "What would create more Alabama interest than to have a get-together to poke fun at the Big Four meeting in France? And what would poke more fun than to ship four strange roosters into Alabama and to display each rooster as representing one of the statesmen meeting in France? We'll get the finest roosters from all over the world and auction them here in Demopolis to raise money for that bridge."

Derby could hardly wait to write Congressman Buck Oliver about "Rooster Bridge" and his plans for the auction. When Congressman Oliver got the letter, he showed it to his good friend, Josephus Daniels, then Secretary of the Navy, but still a newspaper man at heart. Secretary Daniels read Derby's letter and with a chuckle said, "Well, why not? We'll put it over."

Frank Derby's gamecocks were duly acquired in Italy, France, and England, and since the question of national superiority was at stake, the finest specimens were selected for this trip to the U. S. A. The captain of the ship due to make the voyage to New York received instructions that three Very Important Roosters were being consigned to his care. Bulletins were furnished the press from time to time as to how Clemenceau's rooster was standing the trip—as to whether Orlando's rooster was a pearl as usual—as to whether Lloyd George's rooster appeared to be coming down

162

FRAN... ENGLAND ITALY UNITED STATES

President Wilson on behalf of the Big Four presented the roosters to the state of Alabama

with the pip. All items of interest concerning these Very Important Roosters were furnished in bulletins to a waiting press.

As the roosters in their fine cages, national flags flying atop, were lowered to the dock in New York, Frank Derby was there to greet them. They left immediately by special train to Washington, where the President of the United States awaited them. President Wilson on behalf of the Big Four presented the roosters to the state of Alabama to be sold for the benefit of the Dixie Overland Highway. Appearing in the NEW YORK TIMES was a picture of this occasion showing President Wilson joining the laughter that followed a remark that Lloyd George's rooster looked sick.

The day of the auction in Demopolis, August 14, 1919, arrived, and with it more roosters and more people than had ever been assembled in the history of this south Alabama area. In addition to the Big Four, Derby had written to well-known people all over the world, asking them to give a rooster. The response had been so great that the

163

roosters were five thousand strong. Special trains poured in from throughout the state, including one from Montgomery with the Governor of Alabama and members of the senate and the legislature. There were flags and bands and the biggest barbecue that anyone could remember. With forty thousand people present, one day was not long enough to auction all the roosters and eat all the barbecue, and August 15 was just as busy as the day before. Frank Derby had not only proved his ability to corral a crowd, but he had created an hilarious atmosphere in which it was fun to give.

Much amusement was afforded the crowd when Frank Willis Barnett, representing the BIRMINGHAM NEWS, arose to present the rooster which his paper had discovered in a nation-wide search for a "beautiful, proud-stepping bird." Barnett, who was quite an orator, was suitably dressed for the occasion, with spats, stick, and special waistcoat. After dramatically shouting how his paper had secured the healthiest, snappiest rooster in the world to help build the bridge, he lifted the cover from the cage, but the bird was standing weakly on one leg, its sleepy body leaning against the side of the cage, looking as sick as a rooster could. Someone had doped him with morphine. Further amusement was afforded when a small blue hen laid an egg during the auction. As a joke, Helen Keller had sent the hen in place of a rooster. Clemenceau's rooster sold for $10,000, and a group of men from Montgomery bid $44,000 for Wilson's rooster. Over $300,000 was pledged in the two-day auction. A total of $22,000 was made on the barbecue alone.

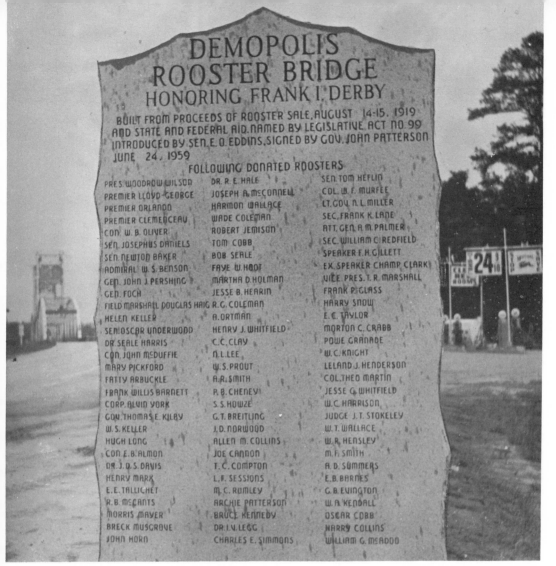

DEMOPOLIS ROOSTER BRIDGE
HONORING FRANK I. DERBY

BUILT FROM PROCEEDS OF ROOSTER SALE, AUGUST 14-15, 1919
AND STATE AND FEDERAL AID. NAMED BY LEGISLATIVE ACT NO. 99
INTRODUCED BY SEN. E. O. EDDINS, SIGNED BY GOV. JOHN PATTERSON
JUNE 24, 1959

FOLLOWING DONATED ROOSTERS

PRES. WOODROW WILSON	DR. R. E. HALE	SEN. TOM HEFLIN
PREMIER LLOYD-GEORGE	JOSEPH A. McCONNELL	COL. W. F. MURFEE
PREMIER ORLANDO	HARMON WALLACE	LT. GOV. N. L. MILLER
PREMIER CLEMENCEAU	WADE COLEMAN	SEC. FRANK K. LANE
CON. W. B. OLIVER	ROBERT JEMISON	ATT. GEN. A. M. PALMER
SEN. JOSEPHUS DANIELS	TOM COBB	SEC. WILLIAM C. REDFIELD
SEN. NEWTON BAKER	BOB SEALE	SPEAKER F. H. GILLETT
ADMIRAL W. S. BENSON	FAYE W. HOOT	EX. SPEAKER CHAMP CLARK
GEN. JOHN J. PERSHING	MARTHA D. HOLMAN	VICE. PRES. T. R. MARSHALL
GEN. FOCH	JESSE B. HEARIN	FRANK P. GLASS
FIELD MARSHAL DOUGLAS HAIG	R. C. COLEMAN	HARRY SNOW
HELEN KELLER	A. ORTMAN	E. C. TAYLOR
SEN. OSCAR UNDERWOOD	HENRY J. WHITFIELD	MORTON C. CRABB
DR. SEALE HARRIS	C. C. CLAY	POWE GRANADE
CON. JOHN McDUFFIE	N. L. LEE	W. C. KNIGHT
MARY PICKFORD	W. S. PROUT	LELAND J. HENDERSON
FATTY ARBUCKLE	A. R. SMITH	COL. THEO MARTIN
FRANK WILLIS BARNETT	P. B. CHENEY	JESSE G. WHITFIELD
CORP. ALVIN YORK	S. S. HOWZE	W. C. HARRISON
GOV. THOMAS E. KILBY	G. T. BREITLING	JUDGE J. T. STOKELEY
W. S. KELLER	J. D. NORWOOD	W. T. WALLACE
HUGH LONG	ALLEN M. COLLINS	W. R. HENSLEY
CON. E. B. ALMON	JOE CANNON	M. F. SMITH
DR. J. D. S. DAVIS	T. C. COMPTON	A. D. SUMMERS
HENRY MARX	L. F. SESSIONS	E. B. BARNES
E. E. TALLICHET	M. C. RUMLEY	C. B. EVINGTON
R. B. McCANTS	ARCHIE PATTERSON	W. A. KENDALL
MORRIS MAYER	BRUCE KENNEDY	OSCAR COBB
BRECK MUSGROVE	DR. I. V. LEGG	HARRY COLLINS
JOHN HORN	CHARLES E. SIMMONS	WILLIAM G. McADOO

This unique landmark lists the names of people who donated roosters

On the Sumter County side of the Demopolis Rooster Bridge in Alabama there stands today an impressive granite marker. This unique landmark, in honor of Frank Derby, lists the names of people who donated roosters in order that a highway obstruction in Alabama would not dishonor the state's name.

Lullabies And Cotton Picking

WHEN Carl Sandburg started compiling material for his book, NEW AMERICAN SONGBAG, he went to Texas to see John A. Lomax, foremost collector of American folklore. There Lomax told Sandburg about Sumter County, Alabama, which he had found richer in folk music than anywhere else in the United States. "In 1936 in Sumter County I made records of 305 folk songs, all from a district of farms covering not more than ten by twenty miles," Lomax told Sandburg. "I know about Sumter County because of Mrs. Ruby Pickens Tartt, who had been recording the Negro songs for the Library of Congress. Without her help I could have made little headway."

Lomax played for Sandburg Mrs. Tartt's recording of "Another Man Done Gone," sung by Vera Hall. Sandburg demanded to hear the recording fifteen or twenty times, and then said, "It is one of the strikingly original creations of Negro singing art. Terror and grief is in the air over a man escaped from the chain gang, a man who killed another man and his name must not be told." Vera Hall was one of Mrs. Tartt's finds. John Lomax's son, Allen, took Vera Hall

Such encouragement has made this small area in southwest Alabama
an invaluable source of folk material

167

to New York, where she gave a concert at Columbia University.

Vera Hall was just one of the many Negroes discovered by Mrs. Tartt. Another one was Harriet McClintock. Mrs. Tartt took Lomax to see "Aunt Harriet," who lived at the top of a steep hill far out in the country. Their car could not make it up the hill so "Aunt Harriet," aged seventy-nine, accompanied by three little grandsons, came down the hill to see them. One of the grandsons carried a rawhide bottom chair for "Aunt Harriet." She sat on the roadside, amiable and smiling, singing into Lomax's recording machine. Lomax, holding a microphone, sat in the dirt road close to "Aunt Harriet" in order not to miss a word of her priceless lullabies and cotton-picking songs.

Enoch Brown was another find of Mrs. Tartt's who provided Lomax with a type of folk song that he had been most anxious to record. One night as he and Mrs. Tartt sat on her porch in Livingston, the quiet of the night was suddenly broken by a long, lonesome, full-voiced call that seemed to come out of nowhere. John Lomax recognized it instantly as one of the "hollows" or calls by which Negroes once communicated from one plantation to the other.

"That's Enoch, crossing the long bridge," Mrs. Tartt said. "He always stops at night in the middle of the bridge and gives that call. I have asked him to come and see you, but he is very shy."

On the following night Lomax had just finished recording several Negro spirituals sung by a church group which had come at Mrs. Tartt's request, when he was aware of a figure in the shadows of a big oak tree. With microphone

OLD COVERED BRIDGE, BUILT 1861
LIVINGSTON, ALA.

"That is Enoch, crossing the long bridge," Mrs. Tartt said. "He always stops at night in the middle of the bridge and gives that call."

in hand, he cautiously approached the figure, realizing that it must be the shy Enoch. Apparently all that Enoch needed was a little encouragement, for he let out with a "hollow" that sent Lomax and his microphone reeling back into the yard twenty feet. Enoch had the most powerful voice that Lomax had ever heard but, by standing several feet from him, Lomax was able to record the almost extinct plantation call.

A different type of folklore was provided by Rich Amerson. Rich was full of talk, and as he spun his folk tales for Mrs. Tartt, Lomax was there to record them. Playing a mouth organ and shuffling his feet, Rich liked best to tell stories about animals that ended in Aesop-like fashion with a moral.

Other noted compilers of folklore made their way to

169

Mrs. Tartt's door in Sumter County. Among these were Elie Siegmeister, Ben Botkin, and Byron Arnold. Folk songs must be sung naturally, and the presence of Mrs. Tartt gained many a stranger his admittance to "foot washings," "baptizings," "wakes," and other occasions. So great is Mrs. Tartt's belief that folklore must be preserved, when she heard of a Negro church that needed a new stove she promised that she would raise the money on one condition—the congregation would promise to continue to sing the old-time spirituals. This they have done.

Such encouragement has made this small area in southwest Alabama an invaluable source of folk material for people all over the United States. Some of the songs Mrs. Tartt has preserved are now being acclaimed by nationally known entertainers. "Another Man Done Gone" sung by Ernie Ford, and "Wild Ox Moan" by Harry Bellafonte, both of them on nation-wide television shows, are proof that Carl Sandburg and John Lomax are not alone in believing that Sumter County in Alabama is this nation's richest area for folk music.

The Night Von Braun Came To Dinner

WORLD famous scientist Dr. Wernher von Braun of Huntsville had a dinner engagement with some high government officials that neither he nor the world plan to forget. It was October 4, 1957. Dr. von Braun's dinner party at Redstone Arsenal in Huntsville included Mr. Neil McElroy, who would be this country's next Secretary of Defense, and Major General John B. Medaris, in charge of the Army Ballistic Missile Agency at Huntsville. Dr. von Braun had said for many years that this country should send up an earth satellite, but the government did not give the idea a full hearing. And now there were rumors that Russia might orbit a satellite of her own, so at the dinner meeting on this particular night Dr. von Braun was more hopeful than ever that America would give him permission to place an object in outer space.

Suddenly, even as it seemed that the satellite subject might never arise, the dinner party was electrified by news that Russia's famous SPUTNIK I, mankind's first earth satellite, had gone into orbit.

"It is a shame," said Dr. von Braun.

"What is a shame?" someone asked.

"This could have been done a long time ago. We ourselves could have orbited a satellite," said Dr. von Braun

"This could have been done a long time ago. We ourselves could have orbited a satellite on October 4, 1955, before the one that the Russians orbited today. But even today our scientific team here at Huntsville lacks permission to do so."

"Then that will be changed," came the answer.

And changed it was. Within a short time Dr. von Braun was given permission to begin firing space probes. Only eighty-three days after SPUTNIK I, he and his Huntsville team of rocketeers launched this country's first earth satellite, EXPLORER I, on January 31, 1958. To the rocket city of Huntsville, Alabama, the date of this January firing was indeed momentous. Huntsville citizens stayed in front of their television and radio sets. Many employees returned that night to the arsenal as interested spectators, because there were direct communications with Cape Canaveral, Florida. The fact that thousands of employees were so interested suggests the high degree of team spirit at Redstone Arsenal.

When at midnight President Eisenhower announced to the world that EXPLORER I was in orbit, Huntsville traffic stopped for jubilant celebrations in the downtown area. Yells, fireworks, and the honking of automobile horns continued late into the night.

Dr. von Braun and his dedicated team deserved such momentous history. These scientists for three decades had been "aiming for the stars." Now they became the team that launched many of this country's most important satellites, followed by the historic flight of the Free World's first astronaut, Alan Shepard, on May 5, 1961. Synonymous with this team that has produced so many satellites are the names V-2 and Corporal, Redstone and Jupiter, and the world's largest known rocket, the Saturn.

Redstone Arsenal, where all this developed, covers 38,781 acres, or more than sixty square miles. Named after the color of rocks around the Huntsville area, the arsenal employs some twenty-three thousand employees and pays them more than 139 million dollars annually. There are thirty-seven thousand employee automobiles registered on the arsenal. More than 160,000 visitors came last year to visit this great enterprise where the land, facilities, and equipment are valued at better than 225 million dollars. Highest

The team has startled the world with its space accomplishments including the Saturn

174

ranking civilian employee on the arsenal is Dr. von Braun, and the highest ranking military employee is Major General Francis McMorrow.

The arsenal began as a Chemical Corps installation in World War II, and since then has seen the adjoining town of Huntsville grow from approximately sixteen thousand to eighty thousand, today's fourth largest city in the state. For many decades, after the state capital was moved from Huntsville in 1820, Huntsville had barely grown. But thanks to the arsenal, Huntsville in recent years has been the fastest growing city in the state, and some have called it the "second fastest growing city" in the nation.

The arsenal has so much distance between its buildings and the firing ranges that the government leases some of the "in-between land" to cattlemen. One can sometimes see cattle grazing in the shadows of giant missiles.

The larger rockets are bolted to the arsenal so that they don't zoom around the Huntsville countryside after they are "test fired." If the Saturn rocket ever tore loose from its bolts, it could fly with part of Huntsville as extra baggage. Only the very small rockets can be tested over a firing range on the arsenal.

Alabama is lucky indeed to claim the von Braun team, one of the most famous scientific groups in history, which has startled the world with its many space accomplishments that go back three decades. This is the team that is helping to bridge the long gap between the famous Indian mounds of Alabama and the stars of outer space.

What A Ride!

WHEN the former German scientists in Huntsville developed a rocket so safe that it earned the nickname "Old Reliable," the government decided this would be the ideal rocket to send our first astronauts into space. Alan Shepard, destined to be our first astronaut, agreed. "Old Reliable" Redstone would be the rocket. And reliable it was. "What a ride!" astronaut Shepard exclaimed with jubilation on May 5, 1961, as he walked again on the "good earth," after his Redstone ride to a record-making height of 115 miles at a speed of 5100 miles an hour.

The Redstone rocket had scored a bull's-eye in launching this country's first astronaut in plain view of the world's television cameras and newspaper reporters. The famous rocket team, formerly with the Army but now with the George C. Marshall Space Flight Center at Huntsville, had proved again that their dedication and experience were more than reliable.

"I think we'll give them all a hand of congratulation," President John F. Kennedy said, praising the Alabama scientists and other United States scientists and technicians

*The Redstone rocket scored a bull's-eye in launching this country's
first astronaut, Alan Shepard*

who helped launch the first American astronaut. Vice-President Lyndon Johnson agreed. "We're glad he went and we're glad he came back," said the Vice-President to hundreds of thousands of people lining the streets to catch a view of the astronaut himself in Washington three days after the Shepard flight. Echoing these words were well-wishers including Virgil I. Grissom, John Glenn, and Scott Carpenter, who within a year would add a one-two-three punch to the space flights begun by Shepard.

On many a clear day, residents of north Alabama can hear the rumble of "ground thunder" and feel the earth tremble under their feet as scientists at Redstone Arsenal experiment with great rockets destined to fly to distant space. It is hoped that on these future flights the passengers, like Shepard, will be so thrilled they too can say: "What a ride!"

"What a ride!" Shepard exclaimed

Alabama Highlights

1540   July 2. Hernando De Soto and his army arrive, to become first white men to traverse Alabama region.
October 18. Battle of Maubila; Tuskaloosa slain.

1541   April 25. Hernando De Soto, after a march through Alabama and many fights with the Indians, discovers the Mississippi River near the present city of Memphis.

1559   De Luna establishes Spanish settlement on Mobile Bay.

1561   Settlement abandoned.

1699   Iberville discovers Massacre, now Dauphin Island.

1702   Bienville builds settlement at Fort Louis de la Mobile, first white settlement in present Alabama.

1704   October 4. The first white child is born on Alabama soil in Mobile. Her name is Jean Francois LeCamp.

1711   Fort Louis de la Mobile moved to present site of Mobile.

1712   La Mothe Cadillac, governor of Mobile; Bienville, lieutenant governor.

1714   Fort Toulouse built near site of present Wetumpka.

1719   Ship *Marechal de Villars,* the De Serigny flagship, lands first shipload of slaves on Dauphin Island.

1720   July 1. Ship *Hercules* lands slaves in Mobile.
Name of Fort Louis de la Mobile changed to Fort Conde la Mobile.

1733   Disastrous hurricane and epidemic sweep Mobile.

1763   Mobile ceded to Great Britain by Treaty of Paris.

1780   March 4. Galvez captures Mobile. City under Spanish rule thirty-
       three years.

1783   Britain cedes United States all territory east of Mississippi except
       Florida.

1786   April 7. William Rufus King is born. This distinguished Alabamian
       would be elected Vice-President of the United States in 1852.

1790   June 1. Colonel McGillivray, called Emperor of the Creeks, heading
       a delegation of Indian chiefs, leaves Little Tallassee near Wetumpka
       for a meeting in New York with President George Washington.

1799   May. Spanish garrison at Fort St. Stephens relieved by U. S. troops.

1800   June. First county (Washington) in Alabama established.

1803   March 8. First cotton gin in Alabama erected at Coosada Bluff, present
       Montgomery County, by Abram Mordecai.
       April 21. Lorenzo Dow, a celebrated preacher, holds religious meetings
       and is the first Protestant minister to preach on Alabama soil.

1807   St. Stephens platted on site of Spanish fort (built about 1788).
       February 19. Aaron Burr, arrested by Captain E. P. Gaines in Wash-
       ington County, returned to Virginia to be tried for treason.

1808   Madison County organized.

1809   Baldwin County organized.

1811   *Mobile Centinel,* Alabama's first newspaper, established.
       August 4. Tecumseh, a Shawnee Indian Chief, comes down from the
       Great Lakes region to preach among Alabama Indians a war of ex-
       termination against the whites.

1812   Madison *Gazette,* second newspaper, established.
       Mobile and Clarke counties organized.

1813   April 15. General James Wilkinson captures Mobile from Spain.
       July 27. The battle of Burnt Corn Creek is fought and American
       forces routed. This is first engagement of the Creek Indian War of
       1813-1814.
       August 30. Fort Mims Massacre; five hundred killed.
       November 12. One of the famous episodes of the Creek Indian War
       occurs. Captain Sam Dale and three companions engage nine Indians
       in a hand to hand fight in a canoe in the middle of the Alabama River

and kill all nine of the Indians. Captain Dale and his companions escape.

December 23. Battle of Holy Ground.

1813-14   Indian wars.

1814   March 27. Battle of Horseshoe Bend; General Andrew Jackson defeats Creek Indians; twenty-year peace follows.

August 9. Creek Indians cede to United States nearly half of present state of Alabama.

1817   Alabama Territory created; William Wyatt Bibb governor; capital, St. Stephens. The name Alabama is from the name of a Southern Indian tribe called Alabamos. The Alabama River was named for the tribe, and from this came the name of the state.

April 22. A large body of French exiles after the fall of Napoleon sail from Philadelphia for Mobile Bay and then the Tombigbee River, where they would settle near the present city of Demopolis.

1818   French Vine and Olive Colony Company, formed by Napoleonic exiles, settles on 92,160 acres of land in Marengo County by Congressional grant.

January 19, First session of territorial general assembly held at St. Stephens.

The first steamboat, *Alabama,* built; makes journey downstream from St. Stephens to Mobile.

Cahaba designated as permanent capital of Alabama.

December 3. The city of Montgomery is chartered.

1819   August 2. State constitution adopted at Huntsville convention.

October 25. First legislative assembly convened in Huntsville.

November 9. William Wyatt Bibb is inaugurated first governor of the state of Alabama at Huntsville, Alabama, then temporary capital of the state.

Dec. 14. Alabama admitted into Union.

1820   William R. King and John W. Walker, first United States senators from Alabama.

July 10. William Wyatt Bibb dies. He was the first and only governor of the Alabama Territory and the first governor of Alabama after it was admitted to the Union in 1819.

September 29. An ad appears in the Huntsville paper offering cotton yarn for domestic use. The textile industry in Alabama may be said to have had its beginning with this cotton yarn plant in Madison County.

December. University of Alabama chartered.

1825 April 3. General Lafayette welcomed at Montgomery.

1826 Seat of government moved to Tuscaloosa.

1827 Disastrous fire sweeps Mobile.

1831 April 19. University of Alabama opened.
First Alabama railroad begun.

1832 Creek and Chickasaw Indians cede to United States all right to territory east of Mississippi.

1833 First canal in Alabama built; Huntsville to Looney's Landing, Tennessee River.
Daniel Pratt builds first plant for the manufacture of cotton-ginning machinery in Autauga County.
November 13. Meteoric shower—when "stars fell on Alabama."

1836 May 16. There is great excitement over gold in Alabama. Miners rush in and found Goldville, Goldberg and Silver Hill, names that speak for themselves. The Goldville community in Tallapoosa County acquires a population of three thousand and the village has fourteen stores, two hotels and seven saloons.
Transfer of Indians to Western reservations begun.

1840 Yellow fever epidemic, 686 die in Mobile; ruinous fire in Mobile.

1841 May 23. Samuel Dale dies. Dale was called the Daniel Boone of the South because of his daring deeds as a scout, guide and Indian fighter during the Creek War of 1813-1814.

1847 December 6. Alabama legislature holds first session in new capital of Montgomery.

1849 December 14. Capitol in Montgomery burns.

1851 Present capitol in Montgomery completed.

1853 Yellow fever epidemic in Mobile kills 764.
March 15. William Rufus King of Alabama takes the oath of office as Vice-President of the United States while in Cuba, where he had gone on account of ill health.

1854 October 3. William Crawford Gorgas is born in Mobile. Major General Gorgas would be credited with making the Panama Canal possible by clearing out breeding places of mosquitoes which carried deadly yellow fever.

1861 State troops ordered to occupy Forts Gaines and Morgan and Mt. Vernon Arsenal.

January 11. Alabama secedes.

February 18. Jefferson Davis, of Mississippi, and Alexander H. Stephens, of Georgia, inaugurated at Montgomery as President and Vice-President of the Confederate States.

April 20. Captain Raphael Semmes is commissioned to the command of the war ship *Sumter,* first Confederate warship to have the honor of flying the Confederate flag.

May 21. Confederate seat of government removed from Montgomery to Richmond, Virginia.

June 30. Admiral Raphael Semmes of Mobile, in command of the warship *Sumter,* the first Confederate warship, steams out of the Mississippi River into the Gulf of Mexico. After an exciting race with the United States man-of-war *Brooklyn,* which was on blockade duty, the *Sumter* would escape to sea and begin to prey on all Federal ships.

1862 Salt famine due to blockade.

1864 July 19. The *Alabama,* a Confederate war vessel of 1040 tons and thirty-two guns commanded by Admiral Raphael Semmes of Alabama, is sunk in a navy duel near Cherbourg, France. For several years Admiral Semmes had roamed the seas raising havoc with Federal shipping.

August 5. Admiral Farragut commanding eighteen Federal war vessels, sails into the pass between Fort Gaines and Fort Morgan to open fire on the two Confederate forts. Admiral Buchanan, commander of the Confederate fleet of four vessels, met the powerful enemy in lower Mobile Bay. The Confederates made a gallant fight but were outnumbered. This was the greatest naval battle of the Civil War.

August 6. Federals take Fort Gaines.

August 23. Federals take Fort Morgan.

1865 April 2. Selma captured.

April 4. Federals destroy University of Alabama buildings.

April 12. Montgomery and Mobile surrender.

May 4. General Richard Taylor surrenders at Citronelle.

May 4-21. Civil government suspended; martial law declared.

1867   March 27. State placed under military law.

1869   April. University of Alabama reopens.

1871   December 19. Birmingham granted charter by legislature.

1872   March 20. Alabama Polytechnic Institute opens at Auburn. (Burned 1887.)
Daniel Pratt and H. F. DeBardeleben begin extensive mining operations.

1873   Cholera in Birmingham.
Yellow fever in Mobile.

1876   Federal troops withdraw from Alabama.

1880   June 27. Helen Keller is born at Tuscumbia, Alabama. Stricken by illness in childhood which left her blind, deaf, and dumb, Miss Keller would become well known all over the world for her work in helping the blind.
November 23. First blast furnace in Birmingham, Alice No. 1, begins operation.

1881   February 10. Tuskegee Normal and Industrial Institute for Negroes founded.
July 4. Booker T. Washington takes charge of the Normal School for Negroes at Tuskegee. The school's name was later changed to Tuskegee Normal and Industrial Institute.

1885   First electric street cars in the South operate in Montgomery.

1886-87 Land boom in Birmingham; lots sell at $1,000 per foot.

1888   March 8. First Alabama steel produced at North Birmingham furnaces and rolled in Bessemer.
December 8. Hawes Riot at Birmingham; thirteen killed.

1892   Alabama Polytechnic Institute becomes coeducational.

1893   University of Alabama opens some courses to women; becomes coeducational in 1898.
General panic, Birmingham boom collapses.

1894   Coal miners strike in northern Alabama, with ten killed in Birmingham.

1895   February 16. The Alabama state flag is adopted by the Alabama state legislature.

1897   July 22. Rolling mills in Birmingham make the first successful experiment in the manufacture of steel.

1898   July 28. The world's largest entire stone meteorite comes to earth near Selma, Alabama. The stone would be placed in the American Museum, New York City.

1908   July 6-August 31. Miners' strike in Birmingham district.

1915   Bone-dry prohibition law adopted.

1917   August 14. 167th Infantry, United States Army, formed from Fourth Alabama to become part of Rainbow Division in World War I.
Camp Sheridan located at Montgomery as mobilization center.

1918   Maxwell Field, Montgomery, designated instruction camp for United States Air Corps.

1923   State Docks Commission created to develop Port of Mobile.

1932   March 21. Tornado kills 315, injures 3,000 in state.

1939   April. Mobile made site of $10,000,000 Army air base.
May. State civil service established.

1941   February. The Bankhead Tunnel under Mobile River opens to traffic. Port of Mobile begins large scale construction of ships for use in World War II; a total of 196 new ships are built and 2,200 repaired.

1943   January 5. George Washington Carver dies. For over forty years he worked at the Tuskegee Institute, experimenting primarily with sweet potatoes and peanuts. He discovered hundreds of products that could be made from these crops.

1944   Gilbertown Oil Field, first successful oil field in Alabama, is discovered.

1946   Luther Leonidas Hill dies. This world-famous pioneer in heart surgery was the first doctor to sew up a beating heart. Alabama's Senator Lister Hill is the son of this noted surgeon.

1952   Senator John Sparkman is candidate for Vice-President of the United States, an unusual honor for Alabama. His Democratic running mate is Adlai E. Stevenson.

1953   October 20. Coliseum opens in Montgomery to become first building of type in world. There is so much space in center, a circus can be shown under its roof.

1958 January 31. This country's first satellite, Explorer I, is launched by the former German team now of Huntsville.

1960 September 8. President Dwight D. Eisenhower comes to Huntsville to dedicate George C. Marshall Space Flight Center, and guests include Governor John Patterson, Mrs. George C. Marshall, and Dr. Wernher von Braun. This event gives formal recognition to Alabama's place in the Space Age.

1961 May 5. A Redstone rocket, produced at Huntsville, launches this country's first astronaut, Alan Shepard, into space.
      July 21. A Redstone rocket, also produced at Huntsville, launches this country's second astronaut, Virgil Grissom, into space.
      October 27. Huntsville's Saturn rocket, heaviest object ever to leave earth, flies from Cape Canaveral, Florida, on a "perfect rocket day." The success of Saturn's eight engines flying together is a "technological breakthrough" in rocketry, and cuts many months off our estimated date for landing on the moon.

1962 March. Dr. Wernher von Braun, world famous rocket pioneer of Huntsville, is requested by the Library of Congress to be represented among its dignitaries, an honor accorded Presidents and other leading American notables.
      May. Former Governor James E. "Big Jim" Folsom, colorful Alabama political figure for many years, is defeated in close race in Democratic Primary as he attempts unprecedented third term.
      June. Representatives from the Alabama area met with United States government officials in Washington and laid plans for United States aid to the University of Alabama Research Institute, a milestone in Alabama technological progress.

187

Styles back then called for strange things just as they do today

For their help the authors are grateful to

DAVID L. DEJARNETTE of Mound State Monument, Moundville; ALYCE BIL-LINGS WALKER of *The Birmingham News,* Birmingham; DR. and MRS. JAMES M. MORGAN, JR., Birmingham; DR. and MRS. HUDSON STRODE, Tuscaloosa; LILLIAN M. MURPHY, Andalusia; JAMES L. DANIELS, JR., ROBERT ALEXANDER SMITH, III, MRS. QUINTINA B. FERRANTI, the Staff of the Huntsville Public Library, ALEX THOMAS of *The Huntsville Times,* Huntsville; GEORGE MERLINI, Fairhope; KATHRYN TUCKER WINDHAM and BEN WINDHAM, Selma; GENEVA STRODE AKENS and DANIEL L. and MARTHA T. AKENS, Atlanta, Georgia; ANGELINE NAZARETIAN, FRANCES C. MURRELL, HADLIE H. CARSON, DR. M. DUBOIS HOWELL, and DR. M. EVELYN MCMILLAN, Athens College, Athens.

H.M.A.

JESSIE HAM, RUTH THORNTON, HELEN STAMPS, Birmingham Public Library, JAMES F. SULZBY, JR., WILLIAM BRANTLEY, LAURA O. FULLER, MARTHA HOOD of *The Birmingham News,* MABEL T. ANDERSON, MARY SUDDOTH, JANE MARX, MRS. JOHN B. COLE, PORTER ELLIS, CLYDE PORTER, ELBERT JOHNSON, NEWTON DEBARDELEBEN, BESTOR BROWN, Birmingham; MARY LYLE LAWSON, Wetumpka; MR. and MRS. W. G. WOOLFOLK, MARY O. MCLEMORE, Montgomery; RUBY PICKENS TARTT, MARTHA WINSTON MITCHELL, DR. ROBERT B. GILBERT, Livingston; GENE FLETCHER THOMAS, Columbus, Georgia; and MARY BOLLING STOKES, Spartanburg, South Carolina. I am especially indebted to ENID B. WINSTON, JANE PORTER NABERS, ANNIE B. MITCHELL, and MARGARET MILLER for many hours of stalwart aid which went beyond the "call of duty."

V.P.B.

189

190

McLean, 36
McLeod, 36
McMillan, 36
McMorrow, Major General Francis, 171
McNeil, 36
McPherson, 36
Memphis, Tennessee, 180
Menowa, Chief, 52
Meridian, Mississippi, 109
Merrimac, The, 134
Meteors, 93-96
Methodist, 93, 126
Middle Ages, 102
Miller, Carl, 22
Milner, John, 104, 139, 145, 148
Mims, Samuel, 45
Mines and Mineral Resources, 104-107, 137-148
Mississippi, 50, 95, 121, 124, 137-138, 147, 181, 183-184
Mississippi River, 25, 29, 89, 180
Mississippi Territory, 36, 57, 65
Missouri, 157
Mobile, 15, 30-34, 46, 75, 104, 106-107, 123, 139, 180-186
Mobile Bay, 29-31, 33, 134-135, 180, 184
Mobile Centinel, 181
Mobile County, 117, 181
Mobile Daily Advertiser, 72
Mobile, Port of, 186
Mobile River, 30-31, 106, 186
Mobile Tribune, 74
Monroe County, 41, 45, 49, 53
Monte Sano, 62, 77
Montgomery, 15, 37, 43, 45, 75-76, 86-87, 97, 99-100, 108-109, 111, 113, 137-138, 141, 143, 159-160, 164, 182-186
Montgomery Commercial Club, 159
Montgomery County, 181
Montgomery Engine and Repair Depot, 160
Moore, General Samuel H., 59-60, 62-64
Moore, A. B., 120
Mordecai, Abram, 181
Morgan, 36
Mound Builders, 17
Mound State Monument Photo, 6, 7, 16
Mound State Monument, 18

Moundville, 15-19
Moundville Indians, 6, 17-18
Moundville priest, 19
Mount Pleasant, 53
Mt. Vernon, 30
Mt. Vernon Arsenal, 184
Murrell, John, 83
Muscle Shoals, 15, 81, 152-153, 155
Muscle Shoals Canal, 153

N

Napoleon, 182
NASA, Marshall Photo, 172, 174, 177, 179
Nashville, Tennessee, 79, 81, 83, 138, 156
Natchez, Mississippi, 65, 81
Natchez Trace, 81, 83
National Bank of Birmingham, 141
National Geographic Society, 22-23
New American Songbag, 166
Newcastle, 145
New Orleans, Louisiana, 34, 81, 84
New Philadelphia, 87
New York, N. Y., 39, 139, 149, 162-163, 168
New York Press Association, 145
New York Times, 163
Nichols, W. S., 103
Nickajack, 109, 113
Norris, John Green, 152
North Birmingham, 185
North Carolina, 102

O

Oklahoma, 89, 91
Old Covered Bridge, 169
Oliver, Congressman Buck, 162
167th Infantry, U. S. Army, 186
Orlando, 162
Orline St. John, 70-71, 75
Oven Bluff, 121
Owen, Marie Bankhead, 100
Owen, Thomas McAdory, 100
Oxmoor furnaces, 145-146, 151

P

Patterson, John, 165, 187
Pensacola, Florida, 38, 41, 43, 46
Perkins, Nicholas, 67, 68
Petticoat Rebellion, 31

194

Tampa Bay, 25
Tartt, Ruby Pickens, 168, 170
Taylor, General Richard, 184
Tecumseh, 45, 181
Tecumseh, The, 134
Tennessee, 50, 81, 109, 113, 116, 153
Tennessee Archeological Society, 21
Tennessee, The, 134, 136
Tennessee River, 81, 90, 183
Tennessee Valley, 79, 94
Tennessee Valley Authority, 21
Tensaw, 15, 45
Texas, 166
Thomasville, 25
Tippecanoe, 97, 99
Tombigbee River, 45, 65, 69, 74, 106, 121, 161, 182
Tory, 37, 114, 116
Trail of Tears, 88, 90-91
Treaty of Paris, 180
Tuskaloosa, Chief, 24-27, 29, 180
Tombigbee-Alabama Area, 48
Tombigbee River, 182
Tuomey, Michael, 107
Tuscaloosa, 15, 90, 99, 106, 128, 139, 180, 183
Tuskegee Normal and Industrial Institute for Negroes, 185-186
Tutwiler Hotel, 161
Twenty-seven Mile Bluff, 30
Twickenham, 58
Tyler, John, 97, 99

U

Union Navy, 134-135
Union Party, 109
U. S. Air Corps, 186
United States Army, 153, 160, 176, 186
United States flags, 115
University of Alabama, 126, 128, 183-185, 187

V

"V-2," 173
Van Buren, Martin, 99

Village Creek, 145
Vine and Olive Colony, 100, 182
Virginia, 68, 80, 121, 181, 184
von Braun, Wernher, 171-173, 175, 187
Vulcan, 148

W

Wakefield, 15, 65
Walker County, 114
Walker, John W., 182
War Between the States, see Civil War
War of 1812, 34-36
Warrior River, 106, 140
Washington, Booker T., 185
Washington County, 65, 68, 117, 120, 181
Washington, D. C., 67, 163, 187
Washington, George, 32, 38, 40, 84, 181
Weatherford, Charles, 43
Weatherford, William "Red Eagle," 42-45, 48, 50-53
Webster's Spelling Book, 56
Wetmore, Colonel Thomas, 101
Wetumpka, 15, 37-39, 99, 180-181
White House of the Confederacy, 144
Wilcox County, 72
Wilkinson, General James, 181
Willett, Colonel Marinus, 39
Wilson, Woodrow, 163-164
Winston County, 114
Winston, John Anthony, 95
Winston, William, 95
World Exposition Fair, 62
World War I, 160, 186
World War II, 175, 186
Worthington, Benjamin P., 141
Wright, Orville, 159-160
Wright, Wilbur, 159-160

Y

Yancey, William L., 111
"Yankees," 62